HULL IMPRESSIONS OF A CITY

JOHN MARKHAM and MARTYN KIRBY

Highgate Publications (Beverley) Ltd.
1991

British Library Cataloguing in Publication Data

Markham, John
   Hull: impressions of a city.
   I. Title
   942.837

ISBN 0-948929-48-0

John Markham and Martyn Kirby thank the many people of Hull who have so willingly contributed to this book.

Gratitude is expressed to Hull Museums and Art Galleries for permission to take photographs in the Hull and East Riding Museum, High Street, Hull.

Published by Highgate Publications (Beverley) Ltd.
2A Wylies Road, Beverley, HU17 7AP
Telephone (0482) 866826

Printed and Typeset by
B.A. Press, Tokenspire Park, Hull Road, Woodmansey,
Beverley, HU17 0TB
Telephone (0482) 882232

Introduction

Hull is many cities. Each of us sees it with different eyes and our view is coloured by many factors — among them, memories, age, experience and way of life. This is a book of impressions, my own in words and Martyn Kirby's in pictures, and because impressions are so subjective it makes no claim or even attempt to be a comprehensive guide to Hull. The choice of topics included is ours and all omissions are deliberate.

A city, like a human being, has its moods, and at different times the same person sees a different Hull. Mornings suit it better than afternoons. It has a freshness and a brightness when the early morning sun is shining and everything is spruced and ready for the invasion of commuters. Then, after a hectic hour, it settles down again, busier than before but still uncrowded — the best of all possible times, with enough activity to be interesting but not to annoy.

As the day goes on, Hull is submerged under the volume of traffic and people, but, once the evening rush hour has waned, a blessed interval of peace descends.

It's a lively, vigorous place on a Saturday morning, but after midday serious shoppers are overwhelmed by weekenders filling in an aimless afternoon, streets become uncomfortably congested and it develops a brashness that has a tendency to turn rather nasty.

It recovers on Sunday morning when the streets come back into their own and you can wander across them in perfect safety and look at buildings you've passed a thousand times but never before noticed.

The changes are not just temporary fluctuations of date and time. Some are deeper and longer lasting. Hull is far more confident and self-assured than it was at the end of the war when courageous defiance had declined into drab uncertainty. When people go on holiday they are no longer embarrassed when they have to admit they come from Hull; instead, they take pride in claiming credit for the Marina and all the other improvements in the city centre.

Some still complain about poor communications, but, secretly, Hull enjoys being a place apart. The E.E.C. has strengthened its Continental links but Hull is not entirely happy at the prospect of losing the luxury of isolation and joining a wider group on equal terms. On the surface, though, it has acquired more European touches, such as multilingual signposts and eating and drinking outdoors, and Humberside Airport and North Sea Ferries have made a journey abroad amazingly easy.

In spite of the current concern about threats to the environment, Hull is a healthier city than it was 40 years ago when Dickensian pea-souper smog, regarded fatalistically as a natural phenomenon of the English climate, periodically brought Hull to a standstill and breathing-in was a hazardous exercise. Clean Air Acts have been so successful in improving the atmosphere that the demarcation between town and country has been blurred, and an incoming traveller passes imperceptibly over the city boundary without the unpleasant onslaught on eyes, nose and throat experienced by those who entered 19th-century Coketowns where black and grey and brown were the obvious shades for clothes which would not 'show dirt', particularly when washing meant a laborious Monday at the dolly tub and mangle. Marks and Spencer have played a major role in creating a brighter Britain and a classless society where dress is no longer an instant indication of income and job.

A clear atmosphere is a bonus for Hull's skyline, an exceptionally interesting and varied one, with roofs of differing ages, styles and levels and some distinctive landmarks. Holy Trinity Church always stands out from the rest: its tower which took so long to build and caused so many problems is as readily recognisable in the oldest pictures of Hull as it is from Paull or from the south bank of the Humber. Not far away are St. Mary's castellations, the Guildhall tower, like the top section of the Empire State Building brought down a bit, and the sparkling bright dome of the new Law Courts waiting to be weathered. The green copper dome of the City Hall would look out of place if it were not so familiar, and such modern mini-skyscrapers as the

The skyline of central Hull showing St. Mary's, Lowgate, on the right and the Guildhall tower in the centre.

Bond Street office block, Essex House in Manor Street, and the College of Further Education in Queens Gardens — still obstinately referred to as the 'Tech', whatever Humberside County Council may decree — are at different stages of acceptance. New buildings tend to jar while they are still novel. But time heals most things; eventually they are taken for granted and only visitors see them with fresh eyes.

Hull's skyline is not as grand as London's, but anyone who stands near Wilberforce monument on a bright summer morning and looks across Queens Gardens to the distant view of the triple-domed Town Docks Museum with the City Hall beyond might feel that London can offer nothing more beautiful.

Most of the impressions conveyed in this book are favourable, but local patriotism cannot blind us to all its faults. Some once-smart areas in the centre have declined from smartness into sleaziness with garishly fronted shops and uninviting eateries which nevertheless do a roaring trade. Hull streets seem to be full of people who are permanently hungry, staving off starvation between meals with cholesterol-packed beefburgers, hot dogs, fish and chips, and other greasy items in moulded containers designed to be dropped once the last morsel has been wolfed. Badly printed out-of-date posters peeling from empty shop windows provide an unlovely contrast to all the improvements, and graffiti is usually too mindless to deserve its posh Italian name. Rail passengers, however, are welcomed by such remarkably cryptic trackside slogans as, 'Milk is Murder', 'Christians Burn Again', and 'Freedom is Anarchy', that they must wonder if they are coming to a city where thought is so profound that it is beyond normal human comprehension.

The Hull accent, one has to admit, is not attractive. Although it's not as difficult to understand or as broad as in some areas, it sounds more like slovenly English than a distinctive style of speech: 't' is often omitted, and 'h' a source of confusion. There are, though, some nice pieces of local dialect which mystify the rest of the country. Hull people 'set' each other home, wait 'while' five o'clock, 'mend fires', and, when they're hungry, 'feel starved' and buy 'patties'. As Northerners they have a talent for dry humour and wry sayings. If a lucky chap fell into King George Dock he would come up with a pocket full of fish, and in the old days those who were really hard up 'couldn't cross Ha'penny Bridge' — the South Bridge on which a toll was levied. Little compassion is shown to those who have 'bugger all up top' and the garrulous are unflatteringly compared to 'a yard of pump water'.

In recent years Hull people have returned to their roots: uncertainty and rapid change make the things that remain more important. They are more likely to wander down High Street, to stroll round the narrow lanes of the Old Town which they haven't visited for years, or to make their way to the waterfront and feel more convinced than ever that they are lucky to live in Hull. They are fascinated with their past and have an insatiable appetite for local history.

The pride they feel is rarely expressed in elegant words. They have little time for fancy phrases, feel superior to those who make a lot of fuss, and despise the high-falutin and the lah-di-dah. Unfortunately the rest of the world is liable to take them at their own self-evaluation and there is a danger that modest understatement causes Hull to be undervalued.

When J. B. Priestley visited Hull in 1933 he found it 'a sound and sensible city, not at all glamorous in itself yet never far from romance'. It was an opinion which, he realised, would annoy 'the typical citizen of Hull, who prides himself upon being a plain and downright fellow'. But Priestley was too wily to be deceived by superficial appearances. The typical Hull citizen 'is not as plain and downright as he would have us believe, and neither is that city of his'.

Hull people are not quite as unbuttoned as they were in 1933 and, in spite of all its tribulations, the city is as lively and vigorous as it ever was. After the Dark Ages has come the Renaissance, and the more Hull proclaims its pride the better for itself — and the rest of the country too.

September, 1991   John Markham

'King Billy' rides against the traffic flow. Cars and people wait their turn to cross the road which takes traffic from the industrial heartland of Hedon Road to the Humber Bridge along Garrison Road.

Watersides

Hull people have always gravitated towards the Pier, not merely for a breath of fresh air but, perhaps, drawn instinctively to the place where the town began, at the corner where the Humber and the River Hull meet. No one with a gene of local loyalty can stand on the raised walkway and look down on the merging of the two rivers and not feel a twitch of pride that an accident of geography has had such momentous consequences. Yorkshire people are accustomed to hiding their emotions, but it is a thrill to be part of that process.

The Old Town may be cramped, but down at the Pier there's a sense of spaciousness, with a great sky overhead and the Humber stretching into the distance past the huge ferries berthed in King George Dock, the cooling tower at Salt End and Paull lighthouse, out into the North Sea and Europe beyond.

When older people reminisce, the talk eventually turns to the Pier. Before foreign holidays were invented Hull children came as close as they could to sea travel by eating their sandwiches and watching the arrival or departure of the New Holland ferry, a pleasure not to be despised by the blasé: seeing a ship leaving home or approaching journey's end is just as exciting whether the voyage is one-mile long or one-thousand.

And there was always unbearably mounting tension as the seconds slipped relentlessly away until the terrifying hooter sent sound waves reverberating through your muscles, always a shock and always louder and more frightening than it had remained in the memory. Hull in the past had a high regard for the Sabbath, and one of the few permitted worldly pleasures was a sedate stroll to the Pier. On Sundays, though, it lacked its famous free side-show: heavy, sweating dray horses led clumping down a steep concrete slope for a relaxing paddle in muddy Humber water.

For a long time after the war the route between Holy Trinity Church and the Pier was a depressing walk past derelict and damaged buildings, untidy businesses and decaying shops and cafés. But it was worth

Looking down Queen Street towards the statue of William de la Pole and the Humber.

experiencing this dreary overture for the terrifying pleasure of climbing to the top deck of the Pier and peering between the planks at the water miles below.

Hull has rediscovered its waterfront. The last ferry has sailed to New Holland and the approach to the pier is a neatly paved piazza for promenading, running about or just staring into the distance towards that fabled shore where, according to legend, the mysterious denizens of South Humberside have their habitations. Even the loos have gone upmarket, lovingly cleaned and made into a lavatorial conservatory by a dedicated attendant who has been publicly honoured for his services above and beyond

Rejuvenated dockside developments. The Marina and its surrounding buildings as seen from the top of Holy Trinity Church.

the call of duty. New housing has brought residents back to the Old Town, and old buildings like the Minerva are as smart as they were seen by artists 150 years or more ago. From a window table in Cerutti's restaurant you can enjoy the best of all worlds on a light summer evening, eating luxurious food and, between mouthfuls, savouring the picturesque marine landscape.

The stretch of the River Hull known as the Harbour was for centuries the focus of trade where ships loaded and unloaded not many yards from High Street on its western bank. Not until the 18th century were the medieval walls replaced by the first of the Georgian docks which were to provide agreeable visions of vessels in full sail moving gracefully past buildings and along streets, right into the heart of the town.

These docks were too far inland for growing needs and larger ships, and later ones were built alongside the Humber. The old town docks were left behind, and the centre of Hull lost that contact with water which it needs as a continuing reminder of its origin and history.

Development of the Marina, like the improvements at the Pier, have created a new role for Humber and Railway Docks and given Hull people a pleasant inducement to visit an area which they had previously been wise to avoid. A colourful Armada of yachts at anchor, brightly dressed amateur sailors doing the things that keep people on boats permanently busy, and sunshine reflected from blue water are all enticingly photogenic. It's a pretty picture, perfect for a calendar. But strong breezes that send the blood supply to your cheeks into overdrive and make walking more of a struggle than it looked from the inside of a car carry the clear message that no invention or technology can overcome the relentless forces of Nature against which generations of Hull men have battled in order to survive.

Marinas, though, are more associated with leisure than livelihood. They exist not by necessity but by choice. Everything looks too pretty to be real, the striped *matelot* sweaters and the designer slacks in pastel shades are too expensive to be genuinely casual working gear, and the manual tasks that keep people occupied are just a pretence that something is happening. It's a world of make-believe, of fantasies fulfilled.

Neverthless, in spite of facetious thoughts that refuse to be suppressed, this is for me the amazing re-discovery and revival of a lost part of Hull, a depressing area, by-passed by progress and almost unknown, given a rare second chance to prove itself.

It seems to be succeeding. Hull has a knack of blending old and new in happy harmony, and from the third-floor balcony of the most expensive room in the Forte Crest Hotel you buy a privileged panoramic view of buildings of all shapes, ages and styles which make their corporate contribution to the character of the city. Across Castle Street is the Earl de Grey, the pub everyone has heard of, with its ornate Victorian frontage and, in total contrast, the complex geometric shapes of Princes Quay, angular, gleaming and glassy, challenging the traditional concept of a building as a box with a roof, but too disturbing for many: I suspect that in a few years it will be regarded with pride. Then Princes Dock Side, famous through an Atkinson Grimshaw painting, with the arched entrance to Trinity House courtyard standing in isolated grandeur among the utilitarian and the nondescript.

Old and new are linked thematically by red bricks: no-nonsense 19th-century warehouses on the opposite side of the road, then, as you slowly turn like an Isherwood camera, new office blocks, houses and apartments, No. 13 converted from its commercial use and now giving residents a grandstand view of a scene that can never be boring, watching two boys watching their fishing rods, wondering about the incomes of the owners of the yachts and the reason they chose such names, watching the bridge open to admit a vessel into the rectangle that was once Railway Dock. Like a Parisian street café, the Marina makes spectators feel pleasurably superior to those being watched — without the need to buy a coffee or tip the waiter.

More of the customary dockland and miscellanea stretching to the Humber forms a backcloth to the Marina, most of it Victorian: a pub covered in vivid green 'bricks', eponymously named, and high Hessle Gate Chambers not far from the spot where Hull's riverside entrance stood when this was a walled town.

The walkway commemorating the Queen's Jubilee that takes you past the Marina, down to the Pier, offers an inviting stroll, though sunshine around here is deceptive and sea breezes blow as strongly as they ever did. As well as the unplanned but artistic pattern of smartly painted yachts at anchor there's an old cannon on a pedestal pointing harmlessly over the estuary, and Hull's Covent Garden market, Humber Street, lapped by water until the area to its south was embanked with earth excavated from Humber Dock, and Nelson and Wellington Streets built and named after current heroes, then, in contrast, a new pub, the

A sea of ships in the Marina.

View of boats and new housing
from the top floor of the
Forte Crest Hotel.

Setting off from the Marina
for another sail on the Humber.

The Spurn lightship now permanently moored in the Marina as seen from
the windows of the Forte Crest Hotel.

Two marines use two mariners in the Marina.

Harbourmasters Tavern, whose controversial design is a more explosive conversation piece than the gun.

Struggling against a strong head wind, you reach the end of the Marina and, as you turn the bend that leads to the Pier, a gale-force breeze almost stops you in your tracks. Cold conditions have always been normal for the people of Hull. They expect life to be hard and even in the Blitz they didn't make a fuss.

On the walkway beside the River Hull we met a Norwegian couple finding their way around with the aid of a map which wasn't always easy to follow.

They were not strangers to the area: the husband was a Grimsby-based engineering manager, particularly interested in industrial architecture. Although impressed by Hull, he thought it had not been as successful as Norwich in blending old and new. He liked Hepworth's Arcade but he was not so happy with Princes Quay.

I tried to dredge up from my memory a local link with Norway. All I could come up with was the information that Queen Maud of Norway had her dresses made by Madame Clapham of Hull. Her Majesty was Madame's most prestigious client and gave her the right to style herself 'Court Dressmaker'. New Theatre-goers often commented on the sign displaying that proud claim hanging outside No. 3 Kingston

The Pease warehouse to the right. The River Hull looking south from Drypool Bridge.

A flotilla of barges collect or deliver from warehouses along the River Hull.

Square as late as 1967. On one occasion, the otherwise invisible husband, Haigh, and Emily Clapham were honoured guests of the King and Queen of Norway in Oslo. I also remembered seeing Norwegian prawns on sale in the Market Hall but it was difficult to turn that fact into an exciting narrative.

After saying goodbye, we met them again in High Street looking for Wilberforce House. It was a sunny morning in early summer, there was little traffic and it was pleasant to stroll. The Norwegian gentleman liked High Street. 'It has,' he said, 'a lot of *esprit*.' No praise is too high for a foreigner who can speak English so fluently that he can, correctly, intersperse a word of French.

Two Norwegian tourists check their guide books against a background of the Tidal Barrier.

The Old Town

The Old Town is at its best on a quiet evening, on a Sunday morning — or any time before the crowds and traffic have arrived or after they have left. Its streets and narrow lanes come into their own when few people are about and a peaceful atmosphere lingers in the emptiness, only lightly disturbed by the sound of your own footsteps. Sentimental souls have invented melodramatic stories of ghosts and secret tunnels but the Old Town needs no fictional fantasies to help it convey the feeling that this is where the story of Hull began.

High Street is a symbol of Hull's tenacity, of its refusal to give in when all the odds are stacked against it. The winding route alongside the river was there at the birth of Hull 800 years ago, and, in spite of bombing in two world wars and the loss of some fine buildings in the second, it manages to retain its character, and more than a hint of romance. Land of Green Ginger is one of the most famous streets in England, not merely in Hull, and large forests have been chopped down to produce the paper on which assorted cranks and 'experts' have aired their theories on the origin of such a strange but lovely name.

Far more interesting and important than academic debates on entymology is the character of the little street and the lanes and alleys round about. On a dark foggy morning the atmosphere is delightfully Dickensian, and memories of *A Christmas Carol* are strengthened by the profusion of lawyers' offices, some bearing the names of long deceased partners.

Nearby lanes and alleyways branch off in various directions and it is here in these quiet backwaters that the spirit of old Hull lives on, by-passed by time. An arched entrance on the west side of Manor Street leads to a narrower and more secluded passage into Parliament Street. It's an unpretentious opening but it is a route through medieval Hull. Reputedly it follows the line of Land of Green Ginger when it curved in a westerly direction towards the Beverley Gate, for Land of Green Ginger was then a section of a major thoroughfare, Beverley Street, which crossed Hull from south to north with this twist in its tail.

A secret Hull is hidden away behind familiar buildings that front the main streets. Bowlalley Lane is a narrow old street, but leading from it there are still narrower passages, The Pathway, through to Alfred Gelder Street, and Exchange Alley which turns a corner and becomes Lowgate Court, with an outlet in Lowgate. This is unknown Hull, little explored, with pleasant old buildings, more interesting than they first appear, like Cogan Chambers, which has a carved staircase, spacious rooms and some nice decorative touches. In its earliest days it was the premises of a major firm of Victorian architects, Smith and Brodrick, responsible for a number of good buildings in the area. More than likely, it was purpose-built to their design.

The giant portcullis of the Tidal Barrier as seen from the top of Holy Trinity Church with cars speeding over the Myton Bridge.
Double yellow lines! No Parking!

Scale Lane. The 'Manchester' was the first ship to dock in Queens Dock. In the centre is what is reputed to be the oldest house in Hull.

The Streets of Hull

The streets of Hull are as mobile as the people who move about them. Some go up in the world, some down. A number, only a shadow of their former selves, endure a humiliating and relentless decline, others an ignominious death.

Albion Street follows the track of a bridle path in the rural outskirts of the walled town, but, from the day that Georgian property developers drew up plans for the first of the elegant terraced houses, it rapidly went upmarket and discarded all traces of its modest origin.

It reached the zenith of its upward progress when it became the fashionable address of affluent residents, their daily needs supplied by servants who occupied the subterranean quarters entered by the area steps. The noble architecture of its major buildings, the palatial Congregational Church and the Royal Institute, earned it the title: the Acropolis of Hull.

Its character now is less grand but more complex. Although it retains enough Georgian style to be noticed, elegance is roughly jolted by stridently modern intruders. A few brass plaques are reminders that for a long time it was the Harley Street of Hull, and lofty apartments where cultured residents once exchanged their comments on the latest lecture at the Literary and Philosophical Society or discussed an editorial in the *Hull Advertiser* or the *Packet* had become the dreaded rooms where patients turned over the pages of a two-year-old *Country Life* and waited for

An aerial view of a great city. The large cupola of the City Hall and triple domes of the Town Docks Museum show up above Princes Quay.

the summons that would send them home reprieved or stunned, as they descended the front steps and walked into an Albion Street forever changed from the one they walked along an hour before.

As for Prospect Street, its name alone is a faint link with the time when it offered a view of the Wolds, while Spring Bank is such a long-established urban thoroughfare that a conscious effort is needed to look at the two words and realise that Hull's water supply once flowed along an open ditch by the side of what was then a country lane.

Pedestrianisation transforms the character of a street. A pretty tiled surface that makes no distinction between footpath and roadway somehow makes a street less serious, a Toytown lane through Leggo buildings, which look quite different viewed from the middle of the road where cars should be and where it always seems wrong to be walking. Being allowed to flout the law creates a sense of unreality.

Queen Victoria Square, on the other hand, has acquired a relaxed Continental air with a colourful flower stall and its spacious piazza surrounded by fine public buildings, grander now they can be seen from a different perspective, unobstructed by traffic. But even an agreeable environment cannot eliminate all

life's problems. I was walking through the square one Monday morning when a man stopped abruptly, looked up at the sky, and screamed, 'Why is the Universe against me?' The rest of us had no answer and pretended not to have heard.

Jameson Street, like Imperial Britain of a few years past, has lost its role and needs to find a new identity. It was planned as a grand approach to Paragon Station and was always a lively street, particularly the western

A refurbished facade in Baker Street.

Elegant Albion Street.

Prospect Street with its shopping centre on the right.

section with its imposing office blocks designed for men confident of their business prospects, the premises of the *Daily Mail*, Miss Thompson's tea shop which the twin-setted ladies of the area had decided was the place to be seen, and two period pieces which in their heyday seemed the height of modernity: the Hollywood Hat Shop for those who wanted to look like their favourite film stars (in those far-off times film stars wore hats), and the chrome and cream bakelite milk bar where you could buy a popular but horrible drink called a milk shake.

Jameson Street managed to hold on to its vitality and its hint of excitement even after the Blitz, all through the long, drab post-war years when rough wooden fences marked the sites where proud buildings had been replaced by a strange amalgam of jagged foundations, decorative floortiles leading nowhere, odd bricks and beams, and flowering weeds released from centuries of restraint. It was still possible to follow the track of Chariot Street, important since Georgian times but almost obliterated. Queens House, built too soon after the war, when architecture was merely adequate, removed all sign of the street, apart from an isolated remnant between Paragon Street and Carr Lane which keeps the old name alive.

Ferensway has never quite achieved the style it promised in its early days as a grand expansive thoroughfare with a name that carried a subconscious echo of Broadway, New York. A symbol of everything modern, it cut its unstoppable way through a maze of slums, destroying the detritus of 19th-century growth. The simple, bold lines of the vast block accommodating the Regal Cinema and the YEB were a visual rejection of traditional designs with all their swags, garlands and sundry irrelevant decorative devices. Ferensway also had its milk bar, a taste of sophistication for the innocent, and Cream Cabs really were cream, another hint of New York City, a place increasingly familiar to Hull's film fans.

Shoppers, however, felt the pull of the older, narrower and more homely streets where businesses with trusted names had been established for generations. Hull was still emotionally attached to the Old Town, and Ferensway remained out on a limb, with vacant sites on either side and all development halted or reversed by the Blitz.

The post-war years dragged on far longer than anyone had ever anticipated but Hull, very gradually, was beginning its westward move towards Ferensway. Twenty-year-old ideas started to achieve reality, though not always in the way that had been intended. Ferensway now is permanently packed with people and traffic. The broad highway is inadequate for a volume of traffic way beyond all expert assessments made in the 1930s, and the street's youthful glamour has faded. The Regal — latterly the A.B.C. — is empty and made more forlorn by peeling posters, and fast-food takeaways have taken Ferensway downmarket.

The grandeur of Charlotte Street, once the finest address in Hull, where Joseph Robinson Pease, the banker, and Charles Lutwidge, Collector of Customs and grandfather of Lewis Carroll resided, was almost extinguished by the 1930s' programme of road improvements that created Ferensway. Only the YPI and its neighbour remain as symbols of faded glory, though they have been annexed by George Street. But, across the road, a characterless section, still called

Hay bales used to cushion Milk Race riders in front of the YPI building in George Street.

Charlotte Street, curves towards the point where the old North Bridge crossed the river: an architectural nonentity, but I would be sorry to see it disappear for it was laid out, then honoured with the name of George III's Consort, in the balmy days of prosperity when Hull burst through its medieval walls and planted posh suburban streets in the fields of Sculcoates.

Ironically (though perhaps appropriately in the wake of social revolution), the name of Charlotte Street Mews, the rear entrance for servants and tradesmen, has proved more durable than that of the superior access at the front intended for their masters and mistresses.

Burden Street, Cross Street, Mill Street and West Street have degenerated into the lowly status of useful short cuts and back entrances to shops, though once they were lively communities in the centre of Hull. In the 19th century those who crowded into the town, believing that whatever hardship they had to suffer could not possibly be worse than what they had left behind, developed Hull's own brand of Cockney chirpiness. They had no choice but to be indomitable, and, with cheerful stoicism, they took the knocks that life continued to hand out.

Unknown Hull: a quiet route from Manor Street to Parliament Street, possibly part of medieval Beverley Street.

On the other hand, some streets have never been more than links between one place and another, though the thousands who use them daily hardly notice their names. New Cross Street between Queens Gardens and Queen Victoria Square only just warrants a separate identity, College Street, off Beverley Road, neither contains an academic institution nor leads to one, and nobody lives in Brandesburton Street (linking Sunny Bank and Spring Bank West): few realise that it was named after the parish whose rector, Dr. John Hymers, left the money which built the college nearby. And there are places like Scott's Square, not too easy to find even when you've been given directions, and Queen's Alley, which you notice only because you're on the look-out for names to add to this list.

As the 20th century nears its end some once important streets like Blanket Row and Blackfriargate linger on precariously, left over from the past. Mytongate has had a lucky escape: Castle Street, now transformed into a dual carriage-way of thundering lorries (and already expansion is in the news), has invaded its territory; the name of Mytongate now survives on a life-support machine with its name attached to a short piece of roadway at the other end of Castle Street; while poor old Popple Street has been almost amputated out of existence. Hull City Council is a merciful body and most streets that succumb to progress are given token compensation when their names are attached to new 'courts' and 'groves' nearby.

Whitefriargate is not what it was. Once upon a time this was a street on the itinerary of every serious shopping expedition. On Saturdays it was packed from side to side, roadway as well as pavement, with people who were not always big spenders but enjoyed being part of the crush and seeing a bit of life. Only back home did they pretend to complain. At Christmas it was at its best, with an infectious cheerfulness which it was impossible not to share, in spite of regular warnings that the person rubbing shoulders with you might be a pickpocket.

Whitefriargate has entered local vocabulary as the benchmark for any place heaving with humanity, and

No town shopping street is complete without buskers. This friendly group is serenading shoppers in Whitefriargate.

everyone understands what is meant when a crowded street in any small town in East Yorkshire is described as 'just like Whitefriargate'. A teacher I once knew who had no other claim to fame was quite witty once in his life when he compared the pleasure of eating in a chaotic school dining hall to the satisfaction derived from a quiet lie-down in the middle of Whitefriargate.

In the early years of this century Whitefriargate established a reputation as the place where things happened. The offices and works of the *Daily Mail* and *Eastern Morning News* made it the focal point for Hull people who, in good and bad times, gathered for spontaneous celebrations or communal support, according to the placards and the latest edition, published as news came in from the big world outside.

It is also one of the few Hull streets given literary immortality: in Winifred Holtby's novel, *Land of Green Ginger*, where she revealed the influence exerted on her by the magical atmosphere of what she called Friarsgate: 'A grey narrow canyon between beetling cliffs. Usually the cliffs are black and grey and angry brown, but at night they blossom surprisingly with orange flowers that leap to light in a dramatic climax of surprise.'

When the age of affluence dawned, the narrow street could no longer cope with the increasing number of vehicles, and Whitefriargate resembled a Red Sea crossing whenever a car edged its cautious way forward through crowds reluctantly shuffling to safety. Pedestrianisation was probably inevitable, and now shoppers may safely gaze from the middle of the street in perfect confidence that they will not be suddenly interrupted by a vehicular assault from the rear.

The reverse side of the coin is that pedestrianisation has removed something fundamental to its character. Whitefriargate has lost its way. It's no longer a street with a purpose, and round Parisian-style billboards are a deliberate touch of frivolity. The average age of strollers has declined. Paving makes it appear broader, and it's now a public area where teenagers gather round seats and think it smart to drink out of cans and display their fluent command of Anglo-Saxon, particularly loudly when they know they can be overheard. Tattoos have increased as fishing and shipping have declined.

It is not all loss. Banning traffic has encouraged buskers, most of them extremely talented, providing cheerful background music: if you don't like it you're not compelled to pay. In the last few hectic days before Christmas emotive tunes and coloured lights revive the heady atmosphere which has always been the hallmark of Whitefriargate in that season.

Whitefriargate, though, no longer has the social mix of its great days when Hull's leading business and professional men were as much part of its everyday life as the masses. The cubicles in the Kardomah Café, where regulars drank a discreet coffee, and the chess boards which made it a gentlemen's club, belong to another world.

Skateboarders making the most of an empty car park off Freetown Way on a Sunday afternoon.

Across the new Stoneferry Bridge with the Clough Road gasometer in the background.

Part of the old building now in the firm's new premises off Garrison Road.

A Spring Bank emergency for the Hull Fire Brigade.

Typical pre-war local authority housing on Marfleet Lane.

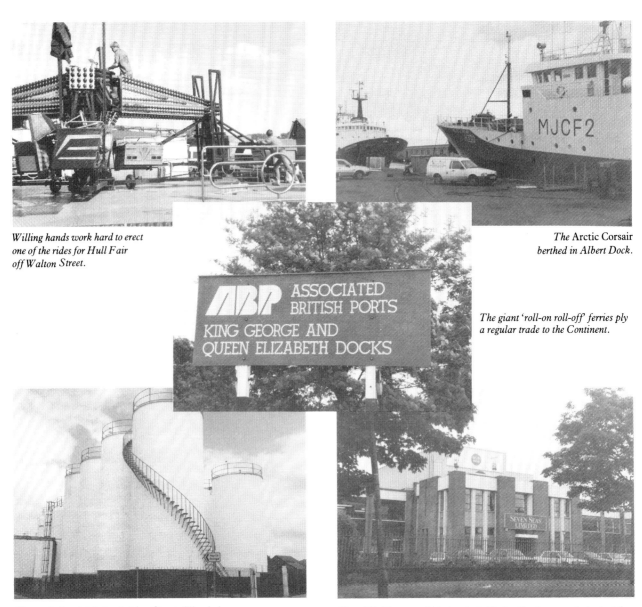

Willing hands work hard to erect one of the rides for Hull Fair off Walton Street.

The Arctic Corsair *berthed in Albert Dock.*

The giant 'roll-on roll-off' ferries ply a regular trade to the Continent.

Elegant industrial design in Lime Street, Wincolmlee.

One of Hull's successful industries in Hedon Road — more important than ever in a health-conscious Britain.

Catalytic crackers at Saltend become a veritable fairyland of twinkling lights at night.

This mock-up 'ship' provides a training base for Humberside Fire Brigade in Priory Way.

It's just over the road!

Giant rolls of paper — a familiar sight on Hedon Road.

The Guildhall, headquarters of the city.

Read all about it!
Selling the Hull Daily Mail *near the Land of Green Ginger.*

The Avenues

Hull has plenty of avenues, but four stand supreme. Mention 'the Avenues' and everyone knows you mean Marlborough, Park, Victoria and Westbourne.

Their unique claim to the title dates from the 1870s when they were named, a period when the word 'avenue' had Gallic novelty and these were intended to attract people concerned about social niceties who wanted to avoid the growing ignominy of living in a street.

In spite of a mobile population, conversions and sub-tenancies, they retain enough permanent residents — some long established — to be a community with a distinctive character. One person who lived there as a child and returned after marriage told me that in summer it has a village atmosphere with the tall trees on either side meeting rurally overhead.

The Avenues are the Hampstead of Hull with intellectuals and progressive thinkers thick on the ground. Stickers and posters advocating current causes and attacking the latest evil in the news block the view from book-lined rooms. A galaxy of famous people who have lived in the Avenues, usually in their pre-fame days, give it added cachet. Dorothy L. Sayers was a lodger, young Ian Carmichael and Amy Johnson lived in their family homes, and Philip Larkin and Alan Plater were there as working residents.

Within the Avenues there is a great diversity of styles. The houses were not contemporaneously produced but built over a period. Some are regarded as pioneering examples of domestic architecture, prototypes of designs which spread in popularity throughout the country. Later owners have provided their own touches of individuality, usually needing an inquisitive pedestrian tour for full appreciation.

Westbourne Avenue has fulfilled its planner's intention of surpassing in grandeur the other three. Its name, with its undertones of Hamlet's undiscovered country from which no traveller returns, is a reminder that the 230-acre site developed by David Parkinson Garbutt, was outside Hull in its early years and was coined to indicate its location with the sprawling parish of Cottingham on its western boundary. A great-aunt who lived to a big age and died years ago told me that, when her grandfather kept cows — in the centre of Hull, not far from the present C&A and Hammonds — he drove them down Spring Bank to graze in the fields where the Avenues were later built.

She could have told me a lot more about old Hull, but I rarely bothered to ask or to listen.

Westbourne Avenue.

The fountain in Westbourne Avenue with typical 'Avenues' houses shown to the left.

Bransholme

So much has already been said and written about Bransholme that it's difficult to see it with unprejudiced eyes.

The first impression of a visitor who had spent the last two decades deprived of all access to the media would probably be of a well-planned development of wide roads and neat blocks of houses, well spaced among green areas, the perfect environment in which to breathe and be happy: the assets which have created many of the problems.

Bransholme was so different from the crowded, cramped streets of Hessle Road, where generations of families had made their home, its unfamiliar openness impersonal and intimidating. Distance lends enchantment to the view, and from the wide open spaces of Bransholme, Hessle Road became the happy land of friendly people, more enchanting as reality receded and nostalgia flooded the memories of those exiled for ever in the bleak flatlands which seemed at the other side of the world, rather than the other side of Hull.

The old houses lacked mod. cons. but the streets and terraces looked alike only to the uninitiated. The sameness was superficial: beneath it a spectrum of individuality, glaringly obvious to anyone who lived there. (Ironically, some of the Bransholme terraces look as if they have been sliced in two — to avoid looking like terraces?) Concrete lacks the colourful warmth of brick, and, if the enveloping greyness of Bransholme dulls the mood of someone like myself merely passing through, it must have a more depressing long-term impact on those who feel it every day.

Large estates — and Bransholme is the largest in Europe — convey the silent, powerfully insidious message that people are all alike with identical needs — a notion that anyone who is human is determined to challenge. Regular rows of units of accommodation communicate the appalling lie that this is what life is like, nothing can ever be different.

With a lot of luck, uniformity will become less apparent and the sense of disorientation that most people feel when cut off from their roots will eventually pass. Communities take time to grow, and, as Bransholme matures into middle age, with leafier trees to soften the starkness of open spaces and protect the people from the threatening emptiness that surrounds them, its unfavourable image should fade. It is still a place without a past. It needs some history behind it so that the next generation can look back to the good old pioneering days and regret that Bransholme isn't what it was.

An example of modern housing on the giant Bransholme Estate.

The entrance to the busy Bransholme shopping centre.

Houses

Number 160 High Street, better known as Maister House, deserves a place in any roll call of Hull's domestic buildings, even though it has long since ceased to be a home.

Its longevity owes more to luck than to local regard for its historical importance, though now that it belongs to the National Trust — the only such property in Humberside — its status is recognised and its future assured.

Built by Henry Maister to replace the timbered house destroyed in 1743 by a tragic fire which killed his wife, his baby son, and two maidservants, trapped by the flames, it was a home for his descendants for only a relatively short period. By the 1820s this influential family which had provided Hull with M.P.s and civic leaders had fallen on hard times. Extravagance, declining business acumen and changed conditions rapidly reduced their status, and the house was abandoned and converted into offices.

Considering its chequered history and the years it was out of bounds to the public, it is probably not surprising that so many local people have never ventured inside. Even during the City's civic weekend when there is a well publicised invitation to visit buildings such as this, quite a number stand on the threshold and peer nervously into the entrance hall, not realising that the great glory of Maister House, the magnificent staircase, is not visible from the doorway. Like other merchants' houses, this was a dual-purpose building. The ground floor was the 'counting house' and the Maisters lived 'above the shop' upstairs: the private section only begins when you have passed

Maister House in High Street — the two Norwegian visitors outside.

Elegant restoration of a Georgian House between Salthouse Lane and Alfred Gelder Street.

A new development in High Street using a variety of bricks, iron work and window designs to achieve interest.

through the hall and turned the corner to face the staircase leading to the family apartments.

Ignorance of such architectural terms as Palladianism, soffits and architraves is no barrier to anyone's ability to appreciate the grandeur of a staircase which is one of Hull's most important artistic treasures. Instead of craning necks, a more sensible way of seeing it in all its glory is to ignore other people's opinion of your eccentricity and adopt a Michaelangelo pose, lying on the floor and looking upward through the well of the staircase to the second-floor gallery and the lantern window which lights it from above.

Those with energy should climb to the top and look down for another stunning view; a door on the first-floor landing leads to a concealed second staircase, far more utilitarian than the one built for ostentatious display to impress upon visitors the prosperity and security of the House of Maister. Sensibly, propertied Georgians did not see any point in spending unnecessarily on decorating staircases seen only by the family on their way to bed or on the backs of furniture which stood against a wall.

Llewellyn Kitchen, one of the two original partners in Gelder & Kitchen, the firm of architects now occupying the building as tenants of the National Trust, is barely remembered today, but his colleague, Alfred Gelder, has one of the best-known names in Hull. Born in North Cave, he became a local celebrity as a member of Hull City Council who became mayor for a record five-year stint, 1898-1903, was knighted and served as M.P. for Brigg. Parliamentary success is ephemeral but Alfred Gelder has achieved as near immortality as Hull can bestow by having a street named after him in honour of his contribution to re-planning the city centre at the turn of the century. A ground-floor room in Maister House containing his roll-top desk is normally out of bounds, but if you have a burning desire to gaze on it you may be able to persuade some kind person to allow you access.

Everyone knows about Wilberforce House: William, the emancipator of slaves, was far more famous than any of the Maisters, and his birthplace has been open to the public since 1906. It has another major advantage over Maister House: a walled rear garden looking on to the river, which may not be a pretty sight with tons of thick brown mud clinging to the timbered props of the Drypool bank, but it is still a waterway to stir the heart of anyone with an affection for Hull. This mud-encrusted stretch of the River Hull was the source of the wealth of the Maisters and the Wilberforces — even further back in time, the reason for the birth of Hull.

Backs of houses are often more revealing than

frontages intended for public view. From the garden side, Wilberforce House discloses more of its complicated structural history. A 17th-century house with traditional screens dividing kitchen and living quarters was re-modelled and enlarged in the mid-18th century by William's father, Robert, who had the means to create a house worthy of the family's elevated social position.

The staircase here at No. 25 is not as grand as the one over the road at No. 160, but it is far too good to be regarded merely as a route to the exhibition rooms upstairs. From a cool marble-floored hall, richly carved balustrades rise to a landing lit by a fine Venetian window, then smoothly turn towards the first floor. The ornate ceiling has been compared to an 18th-century jeweller's snuff box: in its four corners are symbols of the four seasons and at its centre the Wilberforce eagle, all embellished with Rococo scrolls and garlands.

Gloomy museums where reluctant children were dragged to stare in boredom at lifeless objects entombed in glass cases are themselves part of history, and anyone whose knowledge of Wilberforce House is based on a visit made years ago should go again and see how much it has improved. Everything is far more attractively displayed and clearly labelled. The

The lovely Venetian window at the rear of Blaydes House in High Street.

attached Georgian houses form part of the tour and there's quite a lengthy route to follow.

Blaydes House at the northern part of High Street, left out on a limb when Alfred Gelder Street was laid out, has another marble-floored hallway, another richly carved baluster and another Venetian window (this time with a view of the river), for the merchant aristocracy of Hull knew the importance of first impressions.

The grandest room is upstairs in the 18th-century fashion. Blaydes House, which belongs to the Georgian Society for East Yorkshire, is occupied by the architects, Blackmore Son & Co., and the room is used as a drawing office: its ornate doorcase, carved cornice, marble fireplace and fine proportions must provide the perfect working environment for draughtsmen designing modern buildings with subliminal awareness of classical ideals.

Less grand, but a room in which I would be happy to work all day, is one at the rear now used by Mr. Anthony Blackmore. Its uninterrupted prospect of the River Hull was more than an attractive view for the shipbuilding Blaydes, who ran their business from the family house, with a side entrance to the waterside for clerks whose duties and status excluded them from the grand front door, reserved for social equals. It's worth the long climb to the attic for a view over the rooftops of Hull, and a short flight of steps leads to the higher belvedere which enabled the Blaydes (or at least an employee) to survey the Humber with a telescope and obtain valuable advance information about the progress of their shipping.

Hull has its civilised 18th-century terraces in such Georgian suburbs as Albion Street and Baker Street, but inevitably far more housing survives from the Victorian period when population and trade were expanding on a global scale and streets were advancing relentlessly into the rural environs. The top of a bus is a useful vantage point for an illustrated study of the development of Hull. Beverley Road, Anlaby Road, Spring Bank and other major roads follow a general pattern of imposing town houses designed for large, uncontracepted upper-middle class families who could easily afford a full complement of domestics to fetch and carry up and down the long flights of stairs. Houses like these, transplanted to London, would be worth a fortune. They are followed by more demure but still substantial homes, some with vaguely Gothic protuberances, some with anonymous stone faces carved above the front door, and so on, down the social ladder and the decades into the 20th century and the rise of the semi-detached.

Princes Street: an attractive curving row of Georgian town houses.

A rare survival of Georgian working-class housing: Scott's Square off Humber Street.

Wartime destruction and modern in-fillings have, of course, complicated the chronological sequence, and original identities are sometimes buried under typical inner-city conversions of 'front rooms' into shops and business premises. Some have failed; others sccm about to fail; a number have contrived names that strove to be slick but would have been better left uncontrived; and too many have garish facades that look equally appalling whether in pristine state or falling apart.

An extra dimension was added to the outward growth of Hull as offshoots developed on either side, respectable streets of solid, bay-windowed houses, like Coltman Street and Hutt Street, branching off the main roads, then subordinate cross streets which were not such good addresses, and (making totally efficient, economic use of any space available) terraces reflecting each other across tiny gardens linked by a central footpath, humble homes which are now thought important enough for academic researchers to include them in learned tomes as important examples of vernacular architecture.

It was a complex network of inter-dependent cultures, each with its subtle but crucial differences from all the rest. Only to the blind and the insensitive did it appear an anonymous prolitarian mass.

Beverley Road housing. Many substantial houses are now offices.

Renovated houses in Coltman Street which is returning to its former glory.

Varied styles from Victorian Boynton Street to modern Constable Street. Many older houses have extremely decorative doorways.

A leafy lane in Garden Village.

Much has gone. Sometimes new houses have replaced the old; in other places 19th-century buildings survive, too good to die, waiting, not too confidently for a new phase of restoration to their former status. Modernisation has not always been successful, especially misguided attempts to make Victorian property look Georgian by adding 20th-century replica windows and doors. The stages of decline are a blurred but recognisable process, beginning with neglect and disrepair, descending with accelerating pace through multiple or varied usage into the nadir of abandonment and boarded windows. Coltman Street's resurrection is, however, a remarkable example of the way shabby but sound property can be rescued from the abyss.

Flats on Anlaby Road dominate the sky-line. The yawning row of hatchbacks await new owners. Anlaby Road and Witham are the new and used-car centres of Hull.

Bricknell Avenue: a typical suburban development with a wide tree belt in the central reservation.

The new security entrances will hopefully make life safer for the residents of Orchard Park Estate.

The 'Prefabs'. Originally built to last 10 years in the post-war period. Many survive but are being gradually replaced.

'Rooms with a View': new housing along the Humber off South Bridge Road.

Parks

East Park was the most beautiful place I had ever seen: that was my opinion when I was seven. On the way there the bus passed Newtown Buildings (now renamed Newtown Court) and I could imagine nothing more wonderful than living high up in a flat with a balcony. I never noticed the gaol on the opposite side of the road.

I was used to the countryside, but square fields bordered with hedges could not compare with the walk through what seemed an endlessly winding Khyber Pass with flowers creeping through crevices in the massive rocks and a bridge that crossed intriguingly overhead. The sheer size of it all was amazing and, whichever way you went, there was always another surprise round the next bend: among the delights an aviary, an enormous lake, and a water chute that was a thrill even to watch.

I had never heard of Sir James Reckitt, the philanthropic industrialist responsible for the park, or of T. R. Ferens, whose benefactions to his adopted city included the additional land on which the boating lake was dug. It was only in a much later, less innocent, phase of existence that I realised how exceptional Hull was in the quantity and quality of its public gardens. First-time visitors to Hull, expecting a stereotyped northern industrial town of dark satanic mills engulfed in smoke and enlivened only by the clatter of clogs on

The one that got away! The turret from the former Citadel, photographed in East Park where it was located until its recent move to the Victoria Dock area, not far from its original site.

The 'Khyber Pass' in East Park.

Malet Lambert School can just be glimpsed in the centre, beyond the birds, across the lake in East Park.

cobbled streets, often admit their surprise when, instead, they find broad, clean dual-carriage-ways, made positively inviting with trees and flowers artistically distributed among well-tended lawns.

Hull has a long tradition of parks and gardens, dating from 1812 when one of the country's first Botanic Gardens opened, on Anlaby Road (only London and Liverpool had the edge on this pioneering project), and continuing with the idyllically named Strawberry Gardens (in reality rather more noted for their debauchery than their supply of soft fruit), and succeeded by the Zoological Gardens on the site of the previously undeveloped wedge of land between Spring Bank and Beverley Road. Now that the Zoological Pub has gone, only the Polar Bear retains a rather remote link with the pleasure gardens where residents of mid-Victorian Hull were thrilled by firework displays, balloon ascents and what seemed to have been an early form of *son et lumière*, though with more *lumière* than *son*.

All these diversions were available to those who could afford to pay — the Botanic Gardens were a particularly snooty organisation, far too exclusive to admit a mere *servant* in charge of a subscribing member's children — and it was not until 1860 that Hull acquired its first People's Park, open to all, free of charge, the well-publicised gift of the mayor, Zachariah Charles Pearson, a tycoon who revelled in his civic status and in the pleasant sound of popular acclamation of his remarkable munificence. To replenish his apparently bottomless pocket he walked a hazardous tightrope of daring financial deals and finally plunged into the bottomless depths of public disgrace and ruin, Hull's own 'Mayor of Casterbridge'. Pearson was no saint, but time heals most things, and, from the wreckage of his career and the tragedy of his life, Hull retained possession of Pearson Park, a superb legacy from the days when everything he touched seemed to turn to gold.

Designed by James Niven, a landscape gardener of poetic imagination, formerly at Kew and then curator of Hull's Botanic Gardens, it hints at the idealised world of a pre-Raphaelite painting. A lake fringed with trees drooping their branches dreamily into the water curves gently, romantically away. For thirty years after his downfall Pearson lived obscurely in a modest house in a corner of the park which bore his name. On a sunny day, at any time of the year, the park is an attractive oasis of which any city would be proud. When he saw the trees maturing and his vision achieving reality, perhaps bitter memories were occasionally replaced by moments of consolation.

Municipal gardening is often criticised for the Teutonic formality of its flowerbeds, with well-drilled tulips standing to attention in disciplined ranks. Hull parks have avoided the worst of this unlovely style (though a few sternly patterned patches of vivid red and yellow would benefit from an occasional unofficial English rose), and from Pearson Park onwards there has been a successful attempt to broaden the horizons of visitors by landscaping on a far grander scale than anyone could achieve in a suburban back garden.

Like all great cities, Hull is a conglomeration of communities whose members pass in the streets but live in different worlds. Hessle Road residents who never ventured as far as the town centre are legendary, and a lady from a smart area west of Hull was amazed to discover the Garden Village and other interesting features in East Hull: she had been brought up to believe there was nothing worth seeing on the other side of the river.

The green expanses of Pickering Park and West Park's avenue of trees were *terra incognita* to me until I became interested in the story of Hull's public gardens in fairly recent times. Pearson Park I knew only as a short cut from Princes Avenue to Beverley Road when I was at school; I was oblivious of its Victorian charms. The features that once made East Park so appealing are still there, but the magic has vanished, and birds in the aviary look sad and forlorn.

Queens Gardens is a remarkable stroke of luck for Hull, a large central park which any city would give its eye teeth for, and only possible because the port's first man-made dock, a stupendous asset when it was

Pearson Park. The lake.

The imposing gates of Pickering Park's Hessle Road entrance.

Queens Gardens with the Town Docks Museum in the distance.

The ornate and impressive Victorian entrance to Pearson Park.

An avenue of mature trees in West Park.

opened in 1778, was, by the 1930s stranded by progress, and had deteriorated into an irrelevant area of smelly decay, too far inland for the larger ships that used the later docks, developed along the Humber to the east and west.

Conditioned by its rectangular shape and the circumstances in which it was started, Queens Gardens, perhaps inevitably, conforms more to the traditional concept of a municipal garden than the parks which began as wide open spaces on which creative minds could let their imaginations spread. Even so, it is still an attractive example of what Victorians called a 'green lung', surrounded by crowded streets and noisy traffic. For many of us its horticultural beauties are surpassed by the sheer experience of standing half way along the path between Quay Street and Dock Street (the dividing line where a moat-enclosed wall unambiguously separated the thriving town from the rural parish of Sculcoates) and feeling profound admiration for the anonymous and unhonoured Georgian manual workers who, in record time and with no advanced technology, dug out the massive hollow, 1700 ft by 250 ft, piling up the soil on

Going 'walkies' across Costello Playing Fields.

A family day out in Peter Pan Park.

the northern side and so making the ascent to street level steeper there than it is on the opposite side.

It's nicely paradoxical that a garden should be one of Hull's most interesting pieces of industrial architecture. Equally ironic are the gardens created by neglect. Although the wild gardens which brought an unexpected beauty to the wastelands of the war-ravaged city have been smothered by the foundations of new buildings, all over Hull there are colourful patches where yellow ragwort and brilliant red poppies disguise official and illegal rubbish dumps accumulating on areas of coarse, dank grass which wait the arrival of the entrepreneur who will be interested in their financial, rather than their aesthetic, value.

Boy meets girl among the sea serpent scenery of old tyres on Costello Playing Fields.

Hull's Secret Garden

Not too far from the centre is one of Hull's largest — but least known — gardens, now the grounds of Hymers College, though still with unmistakable visual evidence of its late-Victorian glory when it became the suburban successor to the original Botanic Gardens on Anlaby Road, by that time far too encircled by buildings to provide well-heeled subscribers with an exclusive plot where they could stroll amid those specimens of a beneficent Nature which they were fortunate to own.

Once again James Niven had an opportunity of proving that his talent for landscape design had not waned. The new Botanic Gardens had a far more sophisticated layout than any mere expanse of grass relieved by a geometric pattern of mirror-imaged flowerbeds. Anything Nature could do, James Niven could do better, and he devised a variety of delightful walks, a gently curving crescent lake, crossed at its narrowest point by a rustic bridge, and, with a confident eye to the future, planted lavish quantities of trees, bushes and shrubs to create a sensitive counterpoint in shades of green. The drive from the corner where Hymers Avenue and Sunny Bank meet is shown on the original plan of the gardens which hangs in the Headmaster's study, though the lodge — a change of mind or a later building? — appears on the opposite side. The opening of more free parks doomed the grandiosely conceived gardens to a brief period of late Victorian splendour and in 1893 Hymers College opened on the site. Much of Niven's greenery still fringes the school's playing fields. The rustic bridge has gone but in a very dry summer it is possible to trace the outlines of the bandstand and the paths where in the golden sunset of Victoria's long reign straw-boatered gentlemen and parasolled ladies took their refined recreation.

Trying to preserve outmoded features of the past in their pristine state is usually a mistake. A more sensible way of maintaining stability and ensuring continuity is to adapt to new conditions. Although the Botanic Gardens failed to fulfil the dreams of their founders, their inheritance by Hymers College was a splendid stroke of luck: in no other way would so much of real beauty have been preserved. Inevitably private ownership excludes general public access, but schools are not as restrictive and inward-looking as they used to be. There are open days when anyone is free to look round Hymers College and its grounds and there is an excellent view from the Hull-Scarborough railway line.

The house where James Niven resided as curator has been demolished to allow space for new buildings. When I was at Hymers it was used as a flat for a master, a bookstore, and a dining hall where atrocious food was served in the drab post-war years. At that time I had never heard of Niven but I'm now rather pleased to have been inside the house built specially for him.

Hymers College. Students can now look out from Victorian windows across the former Botanic Gardens.

Supermarkets

Those who complain about Hull's supermarkets being impersonal have forgotten, or never experienced, what they replaced.

Corner shops are now viewed nostalgically through spectacles fitted with the thickest of rose-coloured lenses. There was, sentimental raconteurs recall, the cheery chat, the chair by the counter where customers of mature years could rest awhile, savour the excitement of the bacon slicer and exchange merry greetings with neighbours, pass the time of day and hear the latest news of their large circle of friends, for everyone knew everyone else: they were one big happy family. Those were the days when you could pop in as late as you liked for a ha'p'orth of something or other in a triangular paper bag, and the shopkeeper was only too pleased to let you pay when you could.

Coronation Street has preserved in unmelting aspic this image of the friendly neighbourhood corner shop. Rather a sanitised version of reality, though, without the flies and wasps enjoying the sun on their backs as they gambolled among pink-iced yellow-orange buns and lemon curd tarts, vivid glutinous pools trapped by an embankment of impenetrable pastry, all chucked into the window among the crumbs and débris of yesteryear. Aladdin-like interiors about which sentimentalists shed tears were chaotic dumps of cartons, tins, boxes and bottles. Hygienic standards were irrelevant: every inch of the floor and all but a gully on the counter were permanently occupied, while walls were there for hanging displays of cough sweets and constipation cures. The smell was unmistakable though impossible to define, a slightly sweet rotting blend of aromas wafted from fragments of decaying cheese, biscuits, bread and vegetables, lurking undisturbed in inaccessible parts of the shop, accompanied by a hint of oilcloth and linoleum.

Service was excruciatingly slow, and children waited impatiently for uninteresting trivialities to be conveyed, repeated, confirmed, then brought to a fitting conclusion by a suitable platitude, foreseen long before it was uttered. Bitchiness was more apparent than bonhommie.

Supermarkets are a great improvement, but even they have their imperfections. Whichever tiny section of the acres of shelving you need to reach is certain to have its access strategically blocked by a perfectly timed trolley or a stacker. And, even though stackers make a living clumping prices on to packets, the one you choose will have managed to dodge the system. The check-out assistant calls across to her colleague, 'King size Daz, Lynn?' Lynn's answer is never questioned. In a more technologically advanced establishment the question is posed to a microphone and the answer invisibly returned from outer space. Choosing which queue to join requires sophisticated statistical analysis: a single person waiting can deceive the innocent. The contents of the basket — even more the trolley —, the age, gender and personality of the shopper must all be assessed; the merest move towards a cheque book or credit card indicates a journey into another dimension of time. Conversely, a long queue may also give an erroneous impression: it can evaporate as swiftly as the morning dew when a group of four is found to contain only one shopper.

But these are minimal grouses compared with the staggering profusion of products on sale in Hull supermarkets: an almost infinite variety of fruits of the earth, processed and packaged by food engineers as Nature never intended.

The first self-service store I ever entered was in Hammonds' basement in the 1950s, a puny pioneer compared to the vast acres of Asda, Grandways and Tesco spreading into the distance like prairie fields, but just as overwhelming to the easily impressed.

Modern supermarkets have long lines of check-outs, frontier barriers between the worlds of fantasy and reality. Choice is free but bills have to be paid. Seen from a distance in their gleaming, regimental rows, they have the clinical beauty of a geometric design. This may be tomorrow's world but it receives a jolt into the present when a housewife with a reputation to maintain as a good manager studies the payslip intently on the way out. 'It says 29p,' she tells her friend and anyone who's listening, 'but it was a special offer. It should be 25.' She returns to the check-out, a supervisor is called, and people in the queue, realising once again that life is unpredictable, watch while complicated negotiations take place.

Shopping malls, like the Prospect Centre, are bright and clean and purpose-built for customer convenience. Everything gleams and glitters, then gleams and glitters again in reflected glory from shining mirrors, the ritziest suspended from the roof on the sides of shallow, inverted pyramids. From a mini-amphitheatre you crane your neck and look up at the layered interior of the dome or watch the ascent of a glass capsule taking hungry astronauts to the food hall on the floor above.

Nothing is accidental. Nothing happened by chance. This is a place designed by marketing experts to make shopping fun. The idea was perfect on the drawing board but human beings, particularly if they live in Yorkshire, resent being expected to behave according to plan. Fun things produce little real pleasure.

Most streets acquire their character from their haphazardness, an unplanned gradual growth in a variety of styles for a variety of purposes. Shopping is not an activity which ought to be insulated from the rest of life. Commercial apartheid takes it out of its proper context.

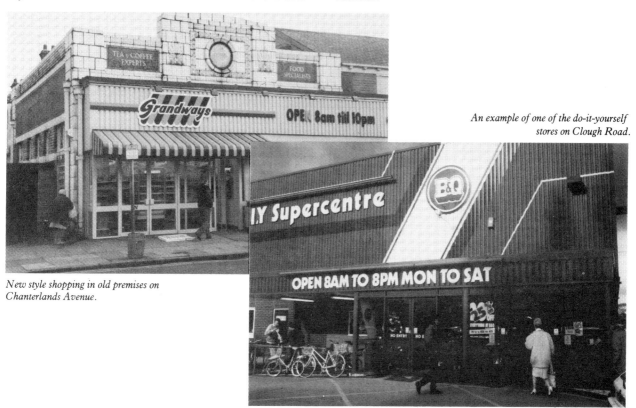

An example of one of the do-it-yourself stores on Clough Road.

New style shopping in old premises on Chanterlands Avenue.

The bustling market in the shadow of Holy Trinity Church.

Markets

The spirit of old Hull flourishes in the market as vigorously as it has ever done from the time when the first traders set up their stalls and bawled out their wares in the shadow of the newly-built Holy Trinity Church: not only vigorously but exuberantly, with mounds of meat piled up in reckless abandon, animal parts spilling out of an overflowing cornucopia sold by well-built stallholders, convincing advertisements for the nutritious properties of the goods on offer.

Meat sold here is far closer to the slaughter house than the poncy products in delicatessens, much touched by human hand, all traces of their animal origin eliminated. There are no tasteless paper-thin slices or genteel packages. Instead, enamel dishes unashamedly loaded with man-size chunks of chopped pork, minced beef, minced tripe, minced lights, pigs' hearts, lamb riblets, spare ribs, belly pork, and slimy chicken pieces, skinned and boned.

Shoppers have to be unshockable and unsqueamish. Rows of plucked wood pigeons rest on their backs with rears exposed and legs pornographically lifted, lusty red kidneys have been hurled in a heap by a frenzied Ripper, and a bowl of liver wobbles obscenely like a chocolate blancmange that has failed to set.

Fruit and vegetables are also closer to the earth, more vigorous, colourful and individual than the standard-size specimens that have satisfied a quality-controller's scrutiny and end up, all neat and tidy, in supermarket cling-film. Pies, pasties, tarts and cakes hardly need to be described as home-made: they were obviously baked

Everybody likes a market! Shoppers scramble for bargains with Trinity House as a background.

A cheerful and stylish welcome greets customers at this busy butcher's stall in the Market Hall.

in an unfitted kitchen by a motherly figure in a flowered pinny, far too experienced to need a recipe book or scales. The pastry has those blimps of individuality entirely lacking in food cloned anonymously in a factory.

People selling, people buying, all realise that they are playing a role. This is not a shop where you wait in a queue and hand your money to a cash-out girl who never looks you in the eye. Here you are expected to join in ritualistic repartee. Everyone is 'love' or 'flower', never 'sir' or 'madam', and every hoary old joke is received with raucous guffaws. A cheeky chappy admits for the hundredth time that he spends most of his life following slow horses and fast women and gives a customer as much delight as if he had coined a scintillating epigram. Another, offering his tatty goods in the open market at ridiculously low prices to a cynically amused crowd who know there's a catch in it, laughs along with his audience when a man at the back shouts, 'They fell off the back of a lorry!'

It is difficult to analyse the distinctive smell of the open market, a combination of smokey grease and raw denim. Hull has never been a clog-clad town, and lace-up boots have been ousted by trainers. Even on the chilliest night a T-shirt and jeans are *de rigeur*, and here

in the open market jeans, bright, faded and deliberately scruffy, are heaped on trestle-tables where thrifty wives and mothers formerly fingered long-lasting drill trousers to test that there was enough spare for letting-out or patching. Another sign of altered attitudes is a notice, 'Changing Room Available', near a piece of hanging carpet which blows revealingly upwards.

One feature provides a continuous link with the beginning of Hull's history. Markets, by tradition, developed at the foot of a church. Hull has had a market at least since 1279, and stallholders clinching a deal in North Church Side with Holy Trinity as a backcloth are part-players in a saga which began 700 years ago and still has many chapters to be written.

The market is a place for older people to revitalise their memories and feel re-assured that nothing important has really changed. For children it is a place of present boredom but an opportunity for storing-up impressions which will become stronger and more valued as time passes. Two grandparents, enjoying every minute, drag a reluctant girl after them, whining, 'Where are we going?'

I know how she feels, but in fifty years she'll be recounting her happy memories to anyone who will listen.

Vast piles of meat in the indoor Market Hall.

It's all here — from wood pigeons to venison!

36

Shopping in the City Centre

King Edward Street is now a walkway and social centre.

Whitefriargate — a magnet for shoppers every weekend.

Hepworth's Arcade — a cool haven for shoppers.

Most Hull people have been in the 'Joke Shop' in Hepworth's Arcade at some time! 'A bow-tie, sir? Certainly. Twirling, squirting or flashing?'

Shimmering reflections. The face of modern shopping seen in Princes Quay.

Princes Quay

Princes Quay is so new that people visit it just because it's there.

First impressions are not necessarily last impressions and, once the superficial novelty wears off, it should come more clearly into focus. At the moment I find the interior overpowering, a Hollywood extravaganza which would suit a large screen but on too vast a scale for human beings walking about the huge stage set like ants. The soaring vaults of great churches rise higher, but they do not diminish the people down below: by showing what man can achieve they elevate their status and raise their aspirations.

As a streamlined medley of shiny, washable surfaces, chromium, Italianate tiles, shimmering metallic strips, mirrored panels, white tubular superstructure, gigantic potted plants and its series of decks overlooking water, it appears to be a cross between a North Sea Ferry, a massive fitted kitchen and the foyer of an international hotel.

Cynics will say that the interior of Princes Quay has one over-riding advantage: the outside is invisible. Instead, there are superb views of Princes Dock Side, an irregular range of interesting old buildings dominated by the arched rear entrance to Trinity House, and plain but pleasant red-brick warehouses.

My own reaction to its overall design is more

Princes Quay — a giant glass ship points its prow towards the Humber. As seen from the tower of Holy Trinity Church.

favourable. Princes Quay is, I think, an exciting addition to Hull's townscape which in time will be regarded more favourably as its merits become apparent. The novelty will also wear off the interior, but whether it wears well remains to be seen.

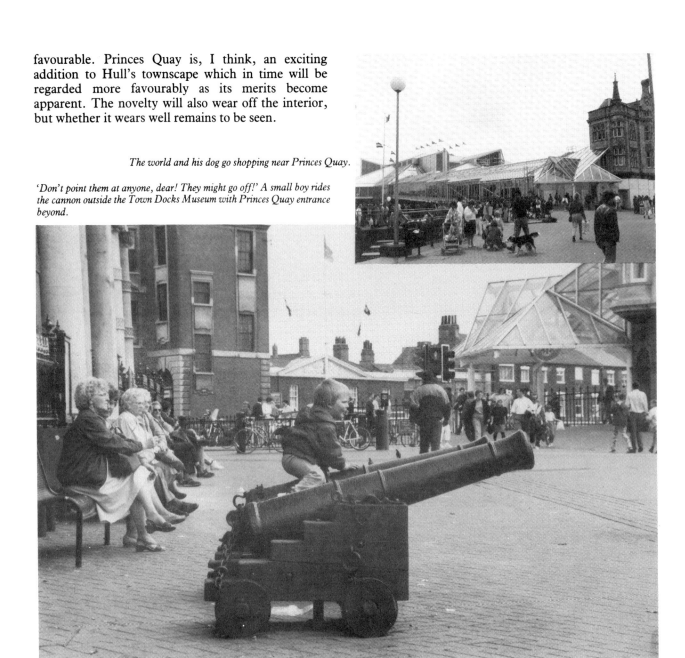

The world and his dog go shopping near Princes Quay.

'Don't point them at anyone, dear! They might go off!' A small boy rides the cannon outside the Town Docks Museum with Princes Quay entrance beyond.

Kingston Square

Kingston Square is at last regaining something of the style to which it was once accustomed.

For long years it faded into dreary decay, like an elderly lady in reduced circumstances who has abandoned all attempt to keep up appearances. The premises where Madame Clapham had demanded total obedience from her slave-driven seamstresses were open until 1967, though in the final 15 years conducted by the heiress niece of the talented but egocentric woman who had miraculously made Hull a centre of fashion. By that time the titled aristocrats and the wives and daughters of Hull's merchant oligarchy had long ceased to arrive in their carriages. The Medical School where young Victorian students attended lectures on anatomy was the Cooperative Institute, and the Assembly Rooms, once the social centre of Hull, had opened inauspiciously in the autumn of 1939 as the New Theatre. It struggled bravely through the Blitz, but in the post-war years an evening isolated among empty seats in such a depressing backwater was hardly enchanting, and the sweetly rotting smell wafted over the Square from Hull Brewery's fermenting hops failed both to stimulate and to inebriate.

Economists rarely have anything useful to say, but in the late 1960s an economist friend predicted that the cheap down-at-heel property of Kingston Square would be a profitable investment: when the drift to the suburbs and the countryside was reversed by a return to more convenient central areas which avoided the

The fine Ionic pillars which grace the New Theatre in Kingston Square.

The former Hull Brewery buildings make a revitalised and well-designed block facing Kingston Square.

The beautifully laid-out park in Kingston Square makes an ideal venue for wedding photographs.

41

twice-daily hassle of commuting, Kingston Square and the streets round about would regain their lost status as good addresses. The prediction has been fulfilled, but the prophecies of an economist are, at best, regarded as interesting though unreliable and I have derived no financial benefit from the prescient advice.

The Medical School has now been demolished, apart from the facade which stands as forlornly as a prisoner under sentence of death, uncertain if delay is a sign of hope or a prolongation of agony. In a far corner, windowless Christ Church school shelters under a temporary roof of fairground-striped tarpaulin, a melancholy memorial to its designer, Cuthbert Brodrick, the most distinguished architect Hull has ever produced.

But the terrace where Emily Clapham exerted her autocratic rule is spruce and bright. Part of her former premises have been converted into the Kingston Theatre Hotel, and Madame's surname has been placed about the entrance to the gaily decorated building. John Street has moved upmarket, and the New Theatre has been given a rejuvenating shot in the arm. Inside, it fizzes with that air of excitement and anticipation which every theatre needs. Externally, it

conveys renewed self-confidence with a stream-lined, glass-fronted balcony bar skilfully slotted between huge Grecian columns. Even the brewery has become an asset since its Cinderella-like transformation into The Maltings.

Kingston Square comes into its own in the evening when people are arriving for a performance, taking a breath of air and a Glyndebourne-style drink at the interval, or trying to find a familiar taxi, car or coach in the melée that gathers outside the theatre from half-past nine onwards.

But it's also a magical place just before Christmas, even on the murkiest and darkest of December afternoons when coloured lights are delicately strung among the bare branches of trees in the central garden no longer reserved for residents.

Spring Street Theatre

It's difficult to write about the Spring Street Theatre without an undertone of unease. There's no doubt that Hull needed a theatre of this type, more flexible and intimate than the proscenium-arched formality of the New, and able to put on less obviously commercial productions. Establishing it was a courageous venture and steering it through difficult times has required real persistence.

On popular nights there is a lively Hampstead-like atmosphere and an intelligent, well-informed audience. But maybe it came too late for me. I feel the odd-one out when everyone else is having a jolly time swallowing the satire and howling at the humour. A readiness to challenge accepted attitudes is fine — until it becomes predictably carping, negative and denigratory. At times there is more than a hint of hypocrisy when sentimental half-truths are accepted as wisdom, or the well-heeled pretend to be proletarians.

Apart from that, I like it.

Kingston Theatre Hotel. Once part of the premises of Madame Clapham — dressmaker to royalty.

Paragon Station

Old-style railway stations were often gloomy places, their 19th-century architectural grandeur darkened by decades of grime and smoke, their basilica-like interiors far too vast for human dramas dwarfed by high glass roofs.

In its latest renaissance Paragon Station has lost many links with its Victorian past, even more than planned when a ferocious fire gutted the interior of the hotel which received the appelation, 'Royal', when the Queen arm-in-arm with Albert, followed by the children they had produced to date and a retinue which included the Prime Minister, processed across the

Paragon Station.

station for a memorable one-night stop on 14 October 1854. Paragon retains the bold sweep of its arched roof but the panelled booking office has permanently closed its hatches and now encases W. H. Smith's bookshop, much more upmarket than the stall where assistants stood behind an open counter. Tickets are now dispensed on miniature turntables from glassed *guichets* in the new Travel Centre, a sort of greenhouse in Disneyland red and green, raised on a terrace.

Everything has been made light and cheerful. No longer is it haunted by the lingering echoes of stiff-upper-lipped goodbyes, ending affairs and brief encounters, altering and sometimes ending lives. The floor has been given a smooth, washable surface that would delight an estate agent: it looks perfect for dislocating the hips of elderly travellers but is probably guaranteed to be slip-free. A flower stall artistically arranged for a production of *My Fair Lady*, and a

'Will it be on time?' Hello and goodbye at Paragon Station.

The familiar 'blue and whites' ready to take passengers to their destinations.

'Glad to be home. Hope the kettle is on!' A weary traveller at Paragon Station.

refreshment bar with the twee name 'Journeys Friend', all subtly suggest that nothing happening here is really serious: a journey by train is a bit of a lark.

Nostalgics will regret the demise of tiny cardboard tickets designed to be lost, the weight machine that provided children of a more innocent age with endless pleasure, Fry's chocolate dispensers which stood tantalisingly empty all through the war and post-war years, and the machine that enabled you to stamp your name on a useless metal strip. The modern equivalent, a mini-studio for photographing a silly expression on your face, is much more sophisticated.

The grime has gone but so has the sense of adventure, the mixture of excitement and apprehension in the air when Paragon was the starting point of a journey into unknown experiences. That atmosphere of anticipation has passed to King George Dock. This is where real journeys begin, not a mere train ride to London in something over two hours but one where you can never become blasé about leaving port, seeing familiar landmarks receding, and knowing that you will wake up in a different world. Gigantic North Sea Ferries tower above everything, visible for miles around while they spend the day in dock, and even

more spectacular when they edge their way delicately through the lock gates with inches to spare. Setting sail is never a dull routine, and anyone standing on shore and watching the great vessel move effortlessly past would, like Wordsworth's traveller crossing Westminster Bridge, be 'dull of soul' if he didn't feel a twinge of emotion.

Even Hull people who keep their feelings under strict control might be persuaded to admit — grudgingly and over a drink — that it's not a bad sight.

A decorative forest of metal enmeshes the Royal Hotel as it rises again from the ashes of a major fire.

The bus station with C & A and Hammonds stores across Ferensway.

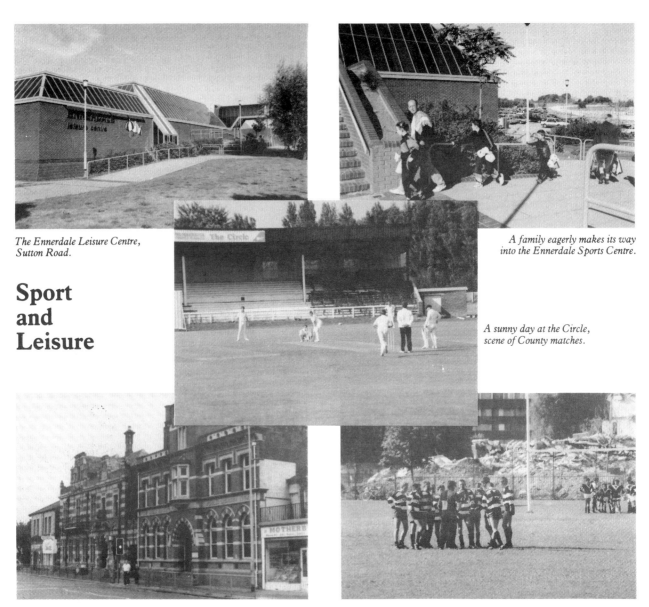

The Ennerdale Leisure Centre, Sutton Road.

A family eagerly makes its way into the Ennerdale Sports Centre.

Sport and Leisure

A sunny day at the Circle, scene of County matches.

East Hull Baths on Holderness Road. A splendid Victorian building with beautiful tiled interior beyond the James Reckitt Library.

Young rugby hopefuls listen attentively in Walker Street. Perhaps they hope to catch the eye of scouts from the 'Airlie Birds' (Hull) or 'Robins' (Kingston Rovers).

Music to sleep by?
In May the Milk Race brings
out people and pandas.

A study in concentration on the
Costello Playing Fields
croquet lawn.

The Milk Race comes to
Queens Gardens.

The Milk Race attracts hordes to Queens Gardens.

The 'lads' enjoying a 'knockabout' on the Costello Playing Fields.

The June regatta makes the Humber a colourful scene.

The Hull Marina attracts boating enthusiasts from far and near.

Bowling enthusiasts on Costello Playing Fields.

Watching the Regatta from Victoria Pier where ferries once left regularly for New Holland.

Regatta day. Crowds cheering the racers in the Humber beyond the basin of the Marina.

Eddie Gray gives professional coaching to young lads at the special Gola Week (Costello Playing Fields). Are there any future 'Tigers' (Hull City) players here?

49

Pubs and Hotels

A yet unwritten best-seller is a book about Hull pubs. There have, of course, been articles and publications galore, but not, so far, the major volume the subject deserves, full of pictures (as many as possible in colour), and looking at the evolution of Hull's public houses within the context of English social and political history as well as examining their architectural styles and eccentricities.

It would be a formidable task. Information is elusive, lurking in unexpected locations, requiring long hours perusing the small print of old newspapers — and quite often non-existent. The search is complicated by frequent name changes, dual names for the same establishment at the same time, and errors both in records and in the memories of happily reminiscing drinkers.

Many pubs have gone, like the Hole in the Wall and Jack on a Raft, but there's a whole catalogue of evocative names still left, a colourful cavalcade of hanging signs and a living link with Hull of a century or more ago. The Blacksmiths Arms, the Brickmaker's Arms, the Engineers Arms and the Whalebone Inn

(near the former Greenland Yards) recall a time when manual workers lived in enclaves not far from their place of employment and drank, often too much and too frequently, in the pub which supplemented chapel and church as a neighbourhood social centre. In those days Father did the drinking for the whole family.

Some pubs recall great people and events, like the Duke of Wellington, the Empress (Queen Victoria

The Dairycoates Inn: a fine example of pub architecture.

The Whittington and Cat with the William Booth Hostel on the other side of Hessle Road.

Where Hedon Road meets Popple Street: once the start of a long thirsty journey into Holderness.

proclaimed Empress of India in 1877), and the Inkerman Tavern (a Crimean battle), though on occasions the origin is forgotten.

The Earl de Grey was High Steward of Hull and a government minister, but his aristocratic title above a well-known pub fails to bring his memory to mind. The Manchester (and its sequel, the New Manchester) has not quite succeeded in keeping alive the fame of the renowned whaler of like name, the first ship to sail into Hull's first dock (later known as Queen's Dock) early one morning in September 1778. The Bonny Boat in Trinity House Lane is not many yards from the 17th-century canoe brought back to Hull and now kept safely among the memorabilia of Trinity House, and it is safe to assume that in the Strickland Arms and the Wassand Arms few glasses are raised to their founding fathers, the Strickland Constables of Wassand Hall, fortunate landowners who built streets on their fields along Hessle Road.

Some famous pubs are now part of the tourist trade, especially those whose names are prefaced by the bogus 'Ye Olde' which no one in the past was ever stupid enough to say: it arises from a misreading of a symbol which looked something like a 'y' but was pronounced 'th'. Pedantry is one of life's little pleasures, and during the course of a guided walk round the Old Town Ye Olde Black Boy provides an opportunity to impart another piece of information: Hull was never a port handling slaves. One inn sign even portrays the wrong monarch: the nearest pub (now closed) to the gilded statue of William III in the Market Place displays a picture of William IV who reigned over a century later.

The Star and Garter on busy Hessle Road.

The Kingston in the shadow of Holy Trinity Church. Dance classes were once held upstairs.

Young and old enjoy the sun and mobile disco at the Brickmaker's Arms on Walton Street.

The Old English Gentleman — where many well-known theatricals have slaked their thirst after a long performance in the New Theatre.

Another apparent regal establishment is the George in Land of Green Ginger, much modernised but still with the evidence of its former existence as a coaching inn. Its sign carries a flattering picture of George IV before over-indulgence ended in monstrous obesity, though the George who gave his name to the inn was no king, merely a saint.

The Old English Gentleman maintains its traditional role as a theatrical pub with signed photographs of the stars and starlets who appeared on the stage of the nearby New Theatre. Modernisation has, however, eviscerated the entrails of old inns throughout Britain, and low ceilings, darkened by decades of strong tobacco smoke, honeycombs of intimate little rooms, and snug alcoves for quiet words in ears have been displaced by large, impersonal multi-purpose bars fitted with juke boxes and fruit machines. Whatever may have happened to their insides, the exteriors of some Hull pubs survive as period pieces, extravagantly, vulgarly ornate, offering a tempting promise of escape from the drabness of daily routine.

Not all changes have been architectural. As well as losing class barriers, pubs have had to respond to female emancipation. The male chauvinism of Ye Olde White Harte and the gentlemen's smoke room in the Haworth Arms, which seemed perfectly acceptable only a few years ago, now appears absurdly antiquated (not unrelated has been the retreat of the middle aged and elderly under the onslaught of T-shirted teenagers and noise levels unacceptable to people in their anecdotage). Microwaved *chilli con carne* and *pizzas* are sold over bars where no landlord who valued his trade would ever have dared offer anything that came within a kilometre of foreign muck. But times have changed. We are now part of Europe!

New public houses have appeared in various parts of Hull in recent years. Most are brand new but two, converted from old buildings, are particularly interesting. The Sailmakers Arms in High Street, traditional in character, dignified in appearance, and approached through an archway leading into a courtyard, looks and sounds as if it had always been an Old Town attraction.

The Institute in Albion Street was a building which seemed destined to a lingering death: well sited and ripe for restoration but moving hazardously close to that fatal stage when all hope is extinguished. And then the miraculous recovery happened. The one-time Albion House, in 1840 the smart new residence of Dr. (later Sir) James Alderson, son of the great Dr. John, had later experienced new phases of life as the Church Institute and the Hull Subscription Library before its resurrection.

It has a strong, formal facade with a weighty portico, entered by a flight of worn stone steps. Inside, more stone steps lead to a large central hall. The conversion has been so radical and so skilful that it is not easy to identify features from the Alderson period, but it works well. Its open plan with galleried bars gives it a spaciousness that is comfortable without being impersonal, and an air of early Victorian grandeur overhangs its imposing iron-balustraded staircase and recessed pillars.

All very different from Victorian beer houses with sawdust on the floors, and spittoons.

Radio Humberside

Local radio and television have developed local pride.

The old-style news, read in solemn southern accents by dinner-jacketed announcers, was always London-oriented, and when Radio Humberside opened in 1971, it seemed strange — almost a breach of etiquette — to hear local people and places mentioned in such a sacrosanct context as a BBC bulletin.

Local radio has broken through barriers of formality and exclusiveness which hedged and hampered the BBC in its early years. It has also made Hull people more aware of the many facets of local life, encouraged a keener interest in local history, and created the links that join individuals into a community.

Broadcasters make a profession of being bright and breezy, but, amazingly, Radio Humberside personalities are just the same off-air as on: amazingly, because all public performances are stressful and by tradition comedians are morose men once the curtain comes down. Radio involves quick thinking, snap decisions, last-minute changes, and coping with the unexpected, all before an audience.

Appearances are often deceptive, and the brains of the Radio Humberside staff may be swirling chaotically while adrenalin pours perilously through the veins, but everyone manages to convey an impression of relaxed efficiency which is infuriating to those of us who never quite achieve it.

It's stimulating to be at the heart of things, and the windows of the top floor newsroom, large, L-shaped and light, with a commanding view of streets in the city centre, is a communication headquarters at the receiving end of information about happenings all over the world, almost as soon as they've happened.

Media people tend to be young and casually dressed, and ties are as rare as surnames. The office is open-plan with constant coming and going and conversations, but there's no suggestion of aimlessness: the work gets done and the programmes go out on time.

This is a building of familiar names but less familiar faces. Peter Adamson, Margaret Garbett, Steve Massam, Liz Meech, Katie Noone and Charlie Partridge were there on the morning we paid a visit. Some look like their voices, others have an audio-image which doesn't quite fit their appearance.

There's a tighter atmosphere on the studio floor below where waiting first-time broadcasters wonder

One well-known voice of BBC Radio Humberside is that of Matt Watkinson, who steers his trusty van to many strange corners of the catchment area to meet the people.

why they ever agreed to come, and look enviously through the glass panel at those who seem to find it no trouble at all. When it's their turn, they'll find it far easier than they ever imagined. Sitting at a table with a microphone is not so different from sitting at a table without a microphone. It comes as a surprise when you find out other people have been listening in to a private conversation.

I've been so polite about Radio Humberside that I'm surely allowed a few words of pedantic complaint to redress the balance: local radio should not make mistakes about local names. Jameson Street, which the studios overlook, is *Jay*meson, not *Jamieson*. Hull University can be called the University of Hull but not *the* Hull University — and the station nearby is plain Paragon Station, not, superfluously, *the* Paragon Station.

The Chapel Street entrance to Radio Humberside. Everyone has a 'tail' to tell. Charlie Partridge (left) and Peter Adamson (right) pay attention to two 'visitors'.

Inside Radio Humberside. Charlie Partridge on the right.

Margaret Garbett, a well-known 'voice' on Radio Humberside.

Blundell's Corner

Putting ideas into words is a mysterious affair, but the process which transforms words into newspapers and books is almost as big a miracle.

Fleet Street, London, has yielded to Wapping, and Hull's Jameson Street has been supplanted by Blundell's Corner as the headquarters of the *Daily Mail* and its associated publications. Traditional printing has also been hurled on to a historical scrapheap by staggeringly versatile technology enabling 60,000 copies to be turned out in an hour and colour to be adjusted from a panel in a control room. The next edition whizzing along above your head in endless sequence is mesmerising, one of those occasions when mechanical repetition creates an abstract pattern more attractive than a lot of modern art.

Rolls of virgin paper, confusingly known in the trade as newsprint, are like gigantic kitchen towels, a ton in weight, brought into Hull from Scandinavia and North Wales and fed into machinery which effortlessly moves from old to new roll with never a second wasted. 140 tons of newsprint in a range of three qualities and a choice of three colours is converted each week into a

The efficient and friendly reception centre at the Hull Daily Mail *building.*

The 'pagoda' style of the Hull Daily Mail *offices at Blundell's Corner is easy on the eye.*

Constructing the local newspaper: one of the colour-co-ordinated offices alive with activity.

Care! A graphic artist at work in the Hi Tec Hull Daily Mail *offices.*

Folded Hull Daily Mails *in a never-ending stream pass up and across to the packing department.*

This control console monitors the details as the thundering presses roll out another Hull Daily Mail.

Loading a roll of newsprint for another batch of Hull Daily Mail.

product which brings good news to some and bad tidings to others.

Everything — apart from the pasting-up of pages — that can be computerised, *is* computerised and video screens are everywhere. Advertising is the financial basis on which editorial content is built: low advertising means smaller papers. Blundell's Corner has a large advertising staff and, after scrutiny, classified advertisements are now keyed direct to the press.

I had always disliked the idea of an open-plan office with its loss of privacy and range of distractions, but the atmosphere here is calm and quiet except for what old-time school inspectors used to praise as the busy hum of activity. It must be difficult to be lazy surrounded by potential spectators, and so many things are happening that they blur into oblivion. There *are* separate sections but they are glass-sided and their occupants like prize specimens in an exhibition. Visiting parties are common and staff take as little notice of the people gawping at them as zoo animals do of the crowds that stand and stare.

In spite of modern technology there is a massive backroom staff. About 450 people are employed at Blundell's Corner in one of Hull's most original new buildings, with interesting low roof lines, situated at a strategic junction where Beverley Road, Spring Bank and Ferensway meet. Inside there is no sign of drama, no one shrieking, 'Stop the presses!', just carpeted corridors and discreet décor — even a glass-enclosed Japanese garden to induce peace of mind. Yet there is not that oppressive sense of isolation from the world outside which permeates some large buildings. This is the right environment in which to produce news-papers.

Blundell's Corner has finally given official recognition to an address which has been part of the Hull vocabulary for well over 150 years, ever since Henry Blundell opened the paint and colour factory which brought wealth to himself, superior conditions to his workers, a major boost to the local economy — and a dominating chimney which forced its way into numerous old photographs. It is a name which should ensure that Hull keeps alive the memory of a man who contributed so much to its growth.

Miles of flying paper flash over and under rollers at the Hull Daily Mail.

The Lord Mayor's Parade

Standing and staring is nearly always enjoyable. Being the one who can watch other people doing things gives you a smug sense of privilege.

The Lord Mayor's Parade is a valiant, fairly new, attempt to establish a tradition and also spread a sense of community by making civic affairs more than a boring phrase. Hull people, though, have lost the talent for spontaneous, innocent celebration of public events so vividly demonstrated when Pearson Park was opened and when Earl de Grey was given the honorific office of Lord High Steward.

Television accustoms us to solitary and private pleasures, and when Martin Prenderleith of Radio Humberside heroically led the 1991 procession on foot, microphone in hand, exhorting us all to fever pitch hysteria, most spectators at the western end of Queens Gardens preferred to remain aloof and unimpressed.

In a following open cream car, travelling at a snail's pace, came the Lord Mayor, wearing a strange bushy hat apparently trimmed with tassels from a 1930s *avant-garde* black lampshade, waving happily and energetically, and accompanied by the Lady Mayoress in a splendid red outfit, far more brilliant than her husband's robe. For some undetectable reason the procession came to a halt. Now, a static procession ceases to make sense, and spectators and the objects of their attention regarded each other with uneasy embarrassment. It was all very informal. People wove their way through the vehicles and the marchers to the other side of the road and, then, suddenly, a casually dressed man left the pavement and walked across to the immobile civic car. There was a second's concern, immediately followed by relief. Hull isn't Dallas — all he wanted was a friendly chat with the Lord Mayor, who seemed delighted to see him. An explosion rent the air but it was only a balloon accidentally touched by someone's grandma's cigarette.

The procession edged forward again. There were inexhaustible supplies of tiny majorettes, an American phenomenon that doesn't transfer comfortably to an English environment. Little girls carrying outsize pom-poms and taking unsynchronised steps are, very independent and not always prepared to display razzamataz. One or two looked distinctly unhappy,

Hull is proud of its many marching bands. Here three trainee 'bandsmen' are coached by their mums.

One of the many floats which made up part of the colourful Lord Mayor's Parade.

with tears not far away, and a woman helper offered a consoling sweet.

Costumed characters on floats waved furiously as they passed but few responded from the crowd: it *is* difficult to generate excitement about Yellow Pages. Some were taking photographs, but video cameras have replaced Box Brownies, and the outfits of the younger spectators owed much to the sartorial influence of *Neighbours:* a bilious patchwork of aggressively clashing stripes, squares and diamonds, day-glow pink in lurid disharmony with acrylic green.

Three youths, indifferent to the civic cavalcade, continued the revolutionary tradition from the spot where Hull rebuffed a king of England yelling the name of the paper they had for sale. But the people walked past, averting their eyes.

The Lord Mayor of Hull rides in style in the Lord Mayor's Parade which is followed by a Gala in East Park.

Churches

Holy Trinity

Churches were intended for large congregations but they are often at their best with few people inside when a tangible presence fills the vacant space. Alone in a great church even an unbeliever must experience spasms of panic difficult to suppress, a sense of something that over-rides rationality. Dusk and darkness encourage long-suppressed emotions to surface, and Holy Trinity Church has an atmosphere gentler and more subdued than during the day, when light streams unhindered through its plain, large windows.

A plain style of worship is also traditional at Holy Trinity, at least since the 17th century when the Puritans of a staunchly Protestant town challenged each other with rival claims that *their* brand of religion was the only one true to the stringent rules eternally writ in Holy Scripture. In the worst days of sectarian strife a wall was built across the church so that the extremist Independents could worship in the chancel while the Presbyterians held *their* services in the nave, often at the same time.

After centuries of acrimonious dispute and thousands of wasted words the angels must have enjoyed a quiet chuckle when they looked down upon Holy Trinity one late spring evening in 1991 and saw the choir stalls filled with people of all denominations listening intently to a talk by the Assistant Roman Catholic Bishop of Middlesbrough and receiving it as sympathetically as a Georgian congregation heard Wesley preach there in the 1780s.

A microphone marginally improved the muffled acoustics, but sincerity cut a clear way through verbal ambiguities. Speaker and audience were safely enclosed in a rectangle of light, with gloom and darkness all around. From time to time an electric bulb gave a sudden symbolic spot of illumination. Through the fussy Victorian fretwork backing the chancel stalls the vague shapes of memorials on the far wall were just about visible.

It was in this church on 30 June 1862 that two of my great-grandparents, John Sales, bachelor, and Hannah Peach, spinster, were married. By all accounts they were highly moral parents who brought up their four children to follow in the paths of righteousness, and

Holy Trinity — the parish church of Hull. Once a daughter church of Hessle. Hull dead had to be carried along the Hessle foreshore, avoiding the tides.

John Sales was the well respected police sergeant in Hedon. Long after their deaths, a birth certificate revealed that on their wedding day they already had a seven-week-old daughter, registered in her mother's surname, Peach, but always known as a Sales. On the south side of Holy Trinity was one of Hull's best-known businesses, the ironmongers, King and Company (now King's Market) which had once been the partnership of King and Peach, a relation of

The Humber and Hedon Road industry framed in the medieval stone parapet on Holy Trinity's roof.

The belfry in Holy Trinity Church contains many mementoes of people and events concerned with bell-ringing.

Hannah, and the name, King and Peach, is still there on the iron pedestals at the four corners of King Billy's statue.

St. Mary's, Lowgate

St. Mary's, Lowgate, is in the centre of the city, passed by a constant stream of traffic, yet it stands quietly and discreetly at the side of the road like a respectable Yorkshire lady who believes in keeping herself to herself.

Its tower is graceful but restrained and, instead of blocking the pavement, concedes a right of way through an arched passage specially cut for pedestrians. The churchyard, angled between the nave and vestry, is small and gloomy, with three trees, one with a massive trunk, overhanging the gravestones packed tightly, head to toe, which were rescued from a drastic Victorian restoration of the interior.

Inside, I'm always reminded of Milton's phrase, 'a dim religious light'. It's a complete contrast to the bright spaciousness of Holy Trinity. St. Mary's is dark

61

and mysterious with a spiritual intensity that lingers in every shadowy corner. Instead of the customary criciform plan, this is a church of idiosyncratic shapelessness, 'a forest of pillars' with no clear demarcation between nave and chancel, stunted by the loss of its western end in the 16th century, and given added girth by an extra aisle tacked on in the 19th.

St. Mary's, Lowgate: a dignified building with a tower walkway to keep pedestrian and traffic apart.

No longer the focal point of a thickly populated parish, St. Mary's is a church with a small but loyal congregation; some members come from quite a distance because they feel the pull of its Anglo-Catholic tradition with its richly textured tapestry of ritual and music.

The finest of its memorials, a Shakespearian-style head and shoulders, honours a merchant, William Dobson, who was so highly regarded in life that his descendants had the temerity to claim: 'We have no reason to doubt his happiness in the next.' Another merchant, Jonathan Beilby, died aged 54, predeceased by his 43-year-old wife, Philadelphia, who had nevertheless managed to give birth to seven sons and five daughters. Particularly well connected was a doctor's wife, Mary Craven, née Welsh, whose name-dropping memorial draws attention to the fact that she was a cousin of Jane Welsh Carlyle (wife of the historian, Thomas), and also a lineal descendant of John Knox.

Surnames like Standidge, Thompson, Thornton and Bannister that once carried great weight in Hull are sad reminders of the unreliability of earthly eminence. Incongruously, in the company of all these worthies is Edward VII, who qualified for a carved head on the choir screen not through godliness but as the monarch in whose reign this piece of ecclesiastical furniture was added.

Memorials are more interesting than architectural technicalities: the people who created a building and gave it life are a vital part of its story, and their influence lingers on.

St. Charles Borromeo

St. Charles has a dramatic interior, an artistic masterpiece of Baroque extravagance which creates an atmosphere found in no other Hull church.

Standing in the sepulchral gloom under the rear gallery and looking across the spiritually suffused shadows of the high-roofed nave towards the crowning

St. Charles Borromeo: the fine central Catholic church in Jarratt Street.

glory, the richly ornate altar where saints float sublimely among clouds, with light descending from above, you could imagine yourself in Austria, never in Hull.

Hanging in an obscure position on the wall of an aisle is a painting of the Nativity, older than the building itself and its most tangible link with the terrors of the past. At the French Revolution it was rescued from a church in Paris by the Abbé Foucher who escaped to exile in Hull and established a Catholic chapel in North Street, where the picture hung as an altarpiece until it was moved across the town when St. Charles was opened in 1829. Marks inflicted by the bayonets of vandalising French Revolutionaries remain on the canvas, not defects but proud emblems, proof of the power of Good to outlive its enemies.

Quaker Meeting House

Vituperative religious differences of past centuries are now blurred by an ecumenical haze, but most churches and chapels in Hull remain undiscovered territory to all but their regular attenders. Even more than pubs and clubs they are a visible reminder that Hull is several places, a federation of communities, each with its distinctive customs and culture.

I knew the Quaker Meeting House in Percy Street from the outside but never had occasion to visit it until this year. A Quaker meeting is so different from a traditional service that it is hardly surprising the room where they gather at 10.45am each Sunday looks nothing like a conventional church. In deliberate disregard of the usual layout, where the congregation sits in rows with eyes to the front like an audience focused on the principal performers, no one here occupies a superior position: there are benches on all four sides of the simple room where the Quakers sit in democratic silence waiting for the Inner Voice to speak to their hearts and perhaps inspire them to pass on the message to other Friends.

It's an austere religion and a demanding one, for its adherents reject the need of any intermediary help of music, minister, regular routine and familiar words, the human ingredients which most of us find an essential emotional and psychological support in our fumbling attempts to bridge two worlds. Inevitably, it appeals only to a minority, though its influence far outweighs the statistical strength of its membership.

As the different denominations have moved towards a common ground, moments of Quaker silence have crept into the services of many churches. Communal silence, however, can create unbearable tension, and

The Quaker Meeting House in Percy Street.

for me, at least, it works only in brief snatches. In longer periods irrelevant and irreverent thoughts crowd into the emptiness.

Religious Choice

Hull has had a stormy religious past and Nonconformist splinter groups which took a different line on some subtle point of theological interpretation from other members of a congregation would set up new chapels where the preaching and worship accorded with their views. So much of this internecine sectarian squabbling now seems pathetically irrelevant, but Hull still offers a remarkable variety of religious establishments to suit all tastes. Architectural styles cover a wide spectrum from early medieval through to functional modernism.

An out-of-the-ordinary church, opened in the middle of the First World War, celebrating its 75th anniversary this year, is St. Mary's, Sculcoates, designed by a notable architrect, Temple Moore, but rarely visited because of its location. It replaced a demolished Georgian predecessor in Air Street, and memorials from the old church were salvaged and brought here. Most curious of all is one in shorthand, and even more visually spectacular is a large gilt wine cooler which doubles as a font.

Just off Beverley Road is St. Anthony's Catholic Church, a bright, colourful modern building with seating so arranged that everyone feels involved and no one sits obscurely at the back, a remote, detached observer of a distant ceremony.

In character it is not so different from the Danish church in Osborne Street, light, friendly and unintimidating, with plenty of the unvarnished Scandinavian wood that features in the décor of many a modern kitchen. It is also a Scandinavian enclave in Hull, a breath and taste of home for exiles who can relax with the pastor and his family and speak their native tongue.

Local people who are honest always admit to the most appalling gaps in their knowledge of the area.

There are many churches I have never visited and many I never will. One regret is never going inside a synagogue. The story of Jewish immigration into Hull is a heroic saga, and succeeding generations have made a great contribution to the City. But the ancient ritual of the synagogue is an aspect of Hull which remains apart from the lives of most of its citizens.

The Danish Church in Osborne Street. A clean, welcoming building for visitors from Scandanavia.

64

Burial Grounds

Philip Larkin found a walk through the melancholy neglect of Spring Bank Cemetery accorded with his pessimistic vision of life, and John Betjeman was entranced by its pseudo-Gothic eccentricities. But churchyards and cemeteries are things from which 20th-century people often avert their eyes, as offended by death as their Victorian ancestors were by the very thought of human sexuality.

Their reaction is not surprising. During a walk through any of Hull's burial grounds intimations of mortality are difficult to keep at bay, and a completely unstatistical survey of the ages of the deceased demonstrates beyond all doubt that living is a precarious activity. Memorials show that in the 18th and early 19th centuries, life could be tragically brief.

But a burial ground becomes more bearable as it ages: the people have receded into the past and become part of history. Old weathered tombstones gently deteriorating under the shelter of tall trees have a symbolism which may not exactly cheer you up but does at least induce a few philosophical reflections.

Holy Trinity's Georgian burial ground is only yards away from the incessantly busy roundabout where Ferensway, Mytongate, Commercial Road and Clive Sullivan Way meet, but it is a tranquil oasis, tidied but not over-disciplined, the last resting place of mothers worn out by bearing children who never had a chance, and of one or two names which have left some mark on local history. The memorial to John Ward, Hull's

The Hull General Cemetery in Spring Bank West: the final resting place of so many of Hull's citizens.

The Spring Bank West entrance to the Hull General Cemetery.

greatest marine artist, has been moved to Trinity House Chapel, but a glass engraver, William Beilby, whose work now commands massive prices in auction rooms (though his own circumstances were not particularly affluent), lies here, rather obscurely, among his family.

The cemetery in Castle Street with the masts of the ships in the Marina visible between the old warehouse and the Forte Crest Hotel. This was the Georgian burial ground for Holy Trinity Church.

Another old churchyard without a church is in Air Street. St. Mary's, Sculcoates, a decayed Georgian church, was demolished in 1916 but the site and the memorials that have survived the elements, and even more ferocious 'restoration', remain as a subdued but not unpleasant green corner in a depressing industrial area. Even so, it is wise not to enter such places unless you have a fairly buoyant temperament. The useful booklets prepared by the East Yorkshire Family History Society enable the timid to read the inscriptions in the reassuring environment of their own home.

This small burial ground was full by 1818 and a new cemetery was opened on the southern side of Sculcoates Lane, a much larger, more impersonal, overwhelming acreage which, in 1890, spread across the road. The East Yorkshire Family History Society has once again undertaken the monumental task of recording all inscriptions. At times they make unbearable reading, human lives distilled into words that a stone can accommodate, the secret history of the people of Hull, providing a silent addendum to the usual accounts of public events and great occasions.

Fine gravestones and rank undergrowth in the General Cemetery, Spring Bank, entranced the poet, John Betjeman.

Burial ground of the former church in Air Street, Bankside. Dr. John Alderson and Dr. Martin Craven are two notables buried here.

One commemorates Augusta Caroline, only child of Captain C. R. Shuckburgh, Staff Officer of the North and East Ridings of Yorkshire, who died in 1844 aged 9 'after a long and painful illness which she endured with exemplary fortitude, patience and resignation'. In 1874 Elizabeth, the beloved wife of George Buck, died aged 18. His anguish scars the verse he had inscribed:

'Sleep on, dear wife and take your rest
For God takes those whom he loves best.
Your youthful days were sweet to me.
Too soon I was deprived of thee.'

Who, I wonder, were the anonymous writers who helped the bereaved express their grief? Some verses are so limpingly amateurish that they sound as if they were the spontaneous outpourings of sorrow. John Leavens' wife, Ann Elizabeth, died in 1851, aged 24, and he mourned her in an epitaph which ends in two poignant unscanned lines:

'I saw her, she was young and fair,
But soon her cheeks grew pale and thin.
Affliction stole the roses there
Wasted the flesh and bleached the skin.
She was but words are wanting to tell what.
Think what a wife should be and she was that.'

A baby son died a few months after his mother.

Some graves were occupied by three unrelated people, and single stones record the names, dates of death, and ages of all three. All had lived at 160 Beverley Road: the address of Sculcoates Workhouse, the castellated red-brick building now absorbed into Kingston General Hospital.

The inmates who died were often the oldest and the youngest, often, too, sharing a grave, George Ryan, aged 72, buried with two infants, George Duke, 7 days, and Dennis Ward, 25 days. Old age brings many unavoidable problems but to survive to the age of 91, like Thomas Carter in 1916, and then end one's days in the workhouse was the ultimate refinement of cruelty which life could inflict.

Dr. Samuel Johnson, who uttered the wry but witty judgment that no man is on oath when he writes an epitaph, would consider his shrewd comment substantiated by some of the older, grander memorials in Hull churches. Human beings are complicated characters, uneasy mixtures of good and bad — or, more often, weaknesses — never quite managing to live up to their ideals. On memorial stones, though, these ordinary mortals are miraculously transformed into perfect wives and husbands, devoted parents, and dutiful sons and daughters. The streets of Hull must have been filled with saints, or, perhaps, to take a kinder view than Samuel Johnson, those who loved them were prepared to overlook the faults and wanted them remembered as they were at their best.

Religion has been a strong force in the history of Hull, but, judging by notices of bereavement inserted in the local press, it would seem that many people in the city hold theological views that would make the Bishop of Durham a paragon of orthodoxy. It has for a long time been a local joke that no one ever dies in Hull: instead, they pass away, fall asleep or, occasionally, receive a call to higher service. A number are clearly annoyed with God for behaving so unreasonably. The clocks in Eternity tick away relentlessly at the same rate as on Earth; and Heaven is a place where people enjoy annual birthday parties. The ideas may be theologically unsound but they are an honest attempt to penetrate the mysteries which have perplexed human beings ever since the first man started to think. Sincerity and love glow through the feeblest, most sentimental clichés, and many are at last able to write the words they were too inhibited to say before.

Statues

King Billy's statue, I find, is now nationally famous.

Visitors to Hull taken on a guided walkabout break into smiles of recognition when they realise that this is where Lucinda Lambton made her ecstatic and privileged descent into the subterranean gents, one of the City's minor delights. The plumbing installation of glass and brass, like goldfish bowls suspended over gleaming tiles to divert the eyes of clients from more immediate concerns, is quaint enough to have produced a whoop of joy from John Betjeman, though it is Edwardian, not the Victoriana it appears.

The king who rides above it all in suspended animation was hardly the dazzling character his gilded equestrian effigy suggests. He was a dour and melancholy man who preferred his native Holland to England, but for Protestant Hull he was a hero, the 'great deliverer', whose accession had freed them from the resented interference of the Catholic James II.

It may not be the greatest work of art but it is certainly eye-catching, and over the years it has attracted more affection from local people than William III could ever inspire in his subjects. From its earliest

days it became a focal point for public events (in 19th-century parliamentary elections poll-toppers earned the doubtful honour of being carried round the statue in a ceremonial chair, assailed by a barrage of insults and missiles), and it is now regarded as a symbol of Hull itself: those who saw King Billy riding out of the Old Town on a lorry at the start of the Second World War to his rural evacuation at Houghton must have witnessed the humiliation and the desertion with heavy hearts.

Hull's tendency to put monarchs over toilets would provide a Freudian analyst with fruitful material for a learned dissertation. Is it perhaps a sub-conscious act of *lèse-majesté*, a tradition which began when Charles I was snubbed at the Beverley Gate, a statuesque lesson in Yorkshire bluntness which makes it clear to those being honoured that, beneath all the trappings of office, they are only human? Or was it that councillors of the past had minds unsullied by levity and never foresaw that some wag would coin the better-than-average riddle, 'Where does Queen Victoria reign over China?'

A more human portrayal of the Queen is the statue in Pearson Park, commissioned by Zachariah Charles Pearson in his days of prosperity but with the sculptor's bill discreetly settled after his financial downfall by Alderman Moss: an unusual statue because it depicts Victoria as a young woman, seated. Not far away another good statue, by the same distinguished Hull-born sculptor, Thomas Earle, commemorates Prince Albert, whose early death devastated his grieving widow and brought genuine sorrow to Hull where the favourable impression he had made on his visit seven years before was still fresh in many memories. A vestigial reminder of popular affection survives in the name of Princes Dock — and now Princes Quay.

Victoria is not the only person to have two statues in Hull. Dr. John Alderson (whose son, James, became the Queen's physician) stands in front of the Infirmary, but a better preserved, more sophisticated one in a toga adds a classical note to the foyer of the City Hall. A plaque records that it was erected by the members of

King Billy rides in golden splendour in the shadow of Holy Trinity.

A youthful Queen Victoria in Pearson Park.

*John Alderson —
the 'Father of Medicine' in Hull.
This statue was
moved from Prospect Street to
Anlaby Road in 1967.*

Prince Albert gazes across Pearson Park with his Queen nearby.

Edward III: the man who put the 'King' in Kingston upon Hull. The marble entrance hall of the Guildhall contains many fine statues of characters in the proud history of Hull.

One of Hull's famous sons, William Wilberforce, in characteristic pose under the shade of trees at Wilberforce House, High Street — not perhaps as well-known as the statue on the column in Queens Gardens.

Our Amy — the record-breaking flights of Amy Johnson are commemorated in Prospect Street.

the Mechanics Institute, an early form of self-help in further education, to commemorate one of Hull's most influential public figures in the struggle to improve the lot of the ordinary people.

The other three City Hall statues are equally interesting and all four are less well-known than they deserve to be. Out of the way on pedestals on either side of the entrance hall, they rarely receive a passing glance from people arriving to claim their seats or rushing out at the end of a performance.

Another great man of Hull, appropriately occupying a secluded corner, as far from the limelight as he always preferred though rarely achieved, is Daniel Sykes, an M.P. of towering morality and steadfast principle, a Reformer too advanced for his constituents. Both Alderson and Sykes were definitely on the side of the angels, but their two colleagues in stone are men who will never be canonised. The heavily bearded patriarch up on his plinth is Anthony Bannister, prominent on the 19th-century Council, and renowned as the promoter of the railway to the coast which transformed Withernsea into a seaside resort. One would guess that he was approaching 80 but he was a civic leader in his thirties and died, probably burnt out, when he was still only 68.

Thrusting Victorian achievers sometimes flouted the ethical codes which the less successful observed. Bannister had his faults but they were mere peccadilloes compared with the downright depravity of his neighbour, James Clay, M.P. In Hull he earned a high reputation as a rousing open-air orator of pre-microphone days — his speeches still read well — and his Radical campaigns made him the hero of the working class. In London he was an habitué of the West End clubs, the country's leading authority on whist, and a man of fashion moving confidently from one social gathering to another. His outstanding characteristic was his insatiable appetite for sex and in his early twenties he had, in the company of the similarly abandoned young Disraeli, made a tour of the Middle East outstanding for the amount of extravagance and debauchery fitted into the itinerary.

Although he posed in Hull as a devoted husband and father, his eldest child was certainly born out of wedlock: so far I have not been able to trace any evidence of a marriage. Clay never left the back benches but he was an exceptionally lucky politician: he lived before the invention of the tabloids and investigative journalism.

The Guildhall foyer is another fine sculpture gallery,

Minerva keeps cool in a High Street garden.

71

though, as passers-by are pre-occupied by more immediate concerns like bills, the busts of Victorian worthies on display are accorded less respect than these men of power and influence had in life. Like the memorial to Ozymandias, they convey an ironic lesson about the transience of earthly fame. John Saner and Charles Wells, big men in their day, survive as street names, and Henry Blundell, one of Hull's industrial princes, a model employer and humanitarian reformer, is remembered more for the corner where his colour factory stood than for his distinguished public career. He was a man of vision, but his unflattering bust, made from a death mask when his eyes were closed, shows him staring blindly into nothingness.

Lord Nunburnholme is fortunate to have such a lofty position in City Square, at the Lowgate end of the Guildhall. Most local people know his statue but there is widespread confusion about his identity. Yet the 1st Baron Nunburnholme, who began life as Charles Henry Wilson, was a power in the family firm, the largest private shipping company in the world, and a Hull M.P. for 28 years — a far stronger claim to fame than hosting a party at which a guest was accused of cheating at cards.

Statues are meant to be stationary, but those in Hull have a habit of whizzing from site to site like hopeful househunters looking for the perfect place where they can finally settle. All the City Hall statues had previous homes, and Michael de la Pole, Edward III (the man who put the King into Kingston), and other assorted dignitaries in the Guildhall have survived unscathed the demolition of the Victorian Town Hall for which they were intended. John Alderson transferred from Prospect Street to the new infirmary, and Andrew Marvell moved from the busy junction of George Street and Jameson Street to a suburban location at the Grammar School in Bricknell Avenue. His future is

Hull's war memorials remind us of those who played their part in the story of Britain.

A giant sized statue of 'Peter' in the old graveyard of St. Peter's, Drypool.

uncertain. The authorities of the Grammar School occupying the former Marist College on Cottingham Road would like him to join them there, now that the Bricknell Avenue school has become the William Gee School: what lawyers call a 'nice' legal point.

When William de la Pole, first mayor of Hull, already moved from his original place of honour in the Victorian Town Hall, became a traffic obstacle in Jameson Street, he was taken to a more symbolic site near the Pier, not far from the two rivers so crucial to the prosperity of himself and the port, ideal for a merchant who may have lined his own pockets but who took Hull a long way with him in his remarkable social and financial progress.

No move, though, has been more remarkable than the re-location of Hull's tallest memorial. William Wilberforce seemed rooted to the spot till the closure of Queen's Dock removed the nearby bridge as an infuriating cause of daily traffic congestion and made removal of the statue itself the obvious next step.

Let's be perfectly clear about one thing: Wilberforce has been moved *once* only. Many local people had a close-up view of Wilberforce when he was supine or in transit. The nearest I have been is the roof of the College which gives a rear view of William, fitted with a lightning conductor and frequently with the humiliation of a pigeon perched on his head which he is powerless to flick away. As far as one can see from the ground, the larger-than-life figure has less individual

The Fishermen's statue on famous Hessle Road looks on as the piebald clops by to pick up another load!

character than the one standing in the front garden of his High Street birthplace.

Statues of the great are out of fashion, and Amy Johnson, one of the 20th-century exceptions commemorated in stone, looks surprisingly bulky on her Prospect Street plinth, though, considering the conditions in *Jason's* open cockpit, her portrayal is probably more accurate than those of earlier celebrities who were idealised as stone supermen after death.

Hull has helped to confuse fact and fiction by erecting a statue to Robinson Crusoe who, only in Defoe's imagination, sailed from the port of Hull. More controversial are the modern works of non-representational art, though the massive fisherman, brooding, chin in hand, over the garden where Drypool church once stood, is a more truthful symbol than older, sentimental pieces which pretended to be realistic.

More genuine, too, than the prissily-named 'street furniture' which has a tweeness only to be expected in something so eager to be noticed. It is, at least, colourful, bright, and evidence of an intention to create pleasure: a pity that the intention is sometimes more apparent than the pleasure. Maybe with the passing of time it will become easier to distinguish between the good and the inferior. Maybe some that are less than perfect will one day be regarded with as much affection as the statue of King Billy, which 18th-century experts dismissed as 'competent but dull'.

A modern sculpture intrigues passers-by as they race along Freetown Way.

Reckitt's

For Hull people Reckitt's — now Reckitt & Colman — has always meant a way of life as much as an industry.

Working at Reckitt's implied membership of an organisation which never considered its responsibilities finished when employees clocked off. The Quaker Reckitts and the Wesleyan Ferens had a paternalistic attitude to their workforce which would now be regarded as undue interference, not only providing welfare facilities (long before they became a state service), continuing education, high-standard housing and a swimming bath, but also doing their damnedest to steer them away from the demon drink.

Reckitt's is literally a household word, even though nowadays few homes ensure they keep a nattily tied packet of Blue ready for the massive Monday wash or for dabbing on when a wasp has struck: Reckitt's Blue is now the only product bearing the family name, but many others have achieved world fame in their own right.

T. R. Ferens, the model moral employee who amassed a fortune and gave most of it away to his adopted city, has also been immortalised in the name of a road, an art gallery, an avenue, a sports ground, and in a little academic joke on the University crest, *Lampada Ferens* — 'Carrying the lamp [of learning]'. Anecdotes about him abound, for people who met him even briefly were conscious of being in the presence of a great man.

Dansom Lane, the main route through Reckitt country, is now closed to the non-Reckitt's public by barriers as impenetrable as the Berlin Wall before 1989. Security is tight in industrial premises all over Hull, and visitors enter Reckitt's under the strictest surveillance.

Externally, the main office block has the architectural style of a university established in the 1920s, though it is, in fact, a post-war building of about 1950, a replacement of its predecessor, destroyed in the Blitz. Inside, it glows with efficient modernity, and Martin Craven, an old friend, took us on a guided tour past a bank and travel bureau into the Business Information Centre, a most up-to-date library but with its archive of original material about the firm and the larger-than-life characters who laid the foundations on which an international conglomerate was to rise.

Upstairs is the directors' palatial sanctum (though also used for special social events) with acres of perfect

The dignified building with a magnificent boardroom for Reckitt and Colman, Dansom Lane.

The first port of call for all visitors — Security Control at Reckitt & Colman.

parquet flooring stretching to the horizon, impressive pillars, tasteful furniture, longcase clocks, and portraits and busts of founding fathers. The company is a world-leader in the late 20th century, but it has never been too busy to keep alive the memory of the 19th-century figures who set it on the road to greatness.

A memorial to Sir James Reckitt in a forecourt has his profile in relief on a pedestal symbolically surmounted by a woman with a hive of bees, epitomising industry which produces its sweet rewards with which to feed her child. The nearby garden of remembrance has as its centrepiece a more romantic tribute (designed by F. Norman Reckitt, Sir James' grandson, who was an architect) to the employees who fell in both Wars. On one side is a quotation from Tennyson:

'Great deeds cannot die
They with the sun and moon renew their
    light,
For ever blessing those that look on them.'

Sir James was a Pacifist and, with a troubled conscience, obeyed the patriotic call of duty in the Great War and turned a blind eye to manufacture of munitions in his factory.

A simple tablet, not far away, lists the men from Dansom Lane and the streets about who joined the forces between 1914 and 1918 as volunteers or conscripts: identical surnames reveal the heavy financial and emotional burden some families had to bear. Its wording is simpler than the literary quotation inscribed on the main memorial but no less moving: 'God Bless Our Boys'.

The early Reckitts and Ferens were living exponents of the Protestant work ethic, a philosophy which contributed so much to the economic prosperity of 19th-century Hull: righteous living and hard work were rewarded by worldly success. Employees had no excuse for forgetting the ethical principles on which the firm was based. A plain building on the site, still known as the Chapel but no longer so used, was opened, according to an obscure plaque, by James Reckitt on 18 September 1876.

It stands only a short distance, though light years away, from the huge modern KWE structure, not spiritually inspired but dedicated to the 20th-century devotion to mild hypochondria. Phenacetin, Lemsip, Disprin and other contents of every health-conscious home are manufactured here.

Prominent on the front is Reckitt & Colman's latest logo, a dramatic explosion of something like streaks of lightning — though still in the traditional blue. Reckitt's are a vital part of the Hull story, linked by a common theme: loyalty to the past but a readiness to adapt to change.

The charming and tranquil Garden of Remembrance at Reckitt's.

Hull Royal Infirmary, Anlaby Road. A major landmark on the Hull skyline since 1967, it replaced the Hull Infirmary built in 1784 on White Horse Ings (now the Prospect Street Shopping Centre) where, in the early days, the stillness was unbroken except for the lowing of herds … and the babble of the Spring Ditch.

Hull Royal Infirmary

A hospital is like L. P. Hartley's definition of the past: it 'is another place. They do things differently there.' It has its own code of behaviour, its own set of values, time moves at a different pace and the important things of everyday life are irrelevant. Patients are quickly conditioned by total immersion in this strange environment where illness and bodily functions are no longer embarrassing topics of conversation but given the prominence they demand.

Visitors, though, apart from the regulars, are afraid of the unfamiliar and try too hard to appear relaxed. They arrive early, as if prompt attendance at the start of visiting hours were compulsory, and in the car park pretend not to stare at others as apprehensive as themselves, trying to read in their faces clues about the condition of the patients they have come to visit.

Few notice the characterless statue in the Infirmary forecourt, but in the memories of some it will surface at unexpected moments as the symbol of a traumatic time. Dr. John Alderson, father of Hull hospital services, weathered by over a century and a half of exposure to the Yorkshire climate, looks blindly away from the towering modern superstructure separated by a medical revolution from his now demolished pioneering premises in George Street and the later 1784 infirmary in Prospect Street, where this statue previously stood.

Once inside, newcomers gaze round the large entrance hall, bewildered by its size and bustle, and conscientiously read the signs. The regulars stroll confidently to the lift, press the right button, then look pityingly at those uncertain what to do who flicker a nervous grin and anxiously watch the indicator changing as the lift whizzes upwards. Regulars are ready to disembark the moment the doors open. Newcomers look at their companions and say, 'Here we are', then stand on the landing longing for help but not daring to ask.

Walking along a corridor and picking out the right patient is the final embarrassment. People in hospital look different; they have the softer, paler faces of individuals protected from the world of competition and supermarket queues. At last they recognise someone they once knew. There is a spendid aerial view of Hull from the windows of the wards but only visitors are interested in the panorama spread out below. It is difficult sustaining a conversation of longer than two minutes, and eagerly pointing out familiar landmarks seen from a new angle helps to pass a few seconds. Patients barely bother to answer politely, for the world outside is no longer their concern.

At the rear of the Hull Royal Infirmary is the severe redbrick annex from a different age of architecture, formerly Western General Hospital but originally Anlaby Road Workhouse, still in use almost 140 years after its opening. A plaque outside records the big-wigs who took credit for this splendid new amenity: the walls are tiled, the stairs of stone, and wards are institutionally long, large and high, all very different from the modern Infirmary and a universe away from the smart new Post-graduate Medical School with its reassuring atmosphere of informed efficiency.

Schools

It is impossible to look objectively at a school you once attended. Solid walls are not as durable as the unaging people who eternally re-enact their classroom roles and repeat the words which no one can change. Hull schools fall chronologically into three main categories: Victorian, inter-war and postwar, but for former pupils — and teachers — architectural history is far less important than the things that happened inside.

Victorian Board Schools were so formidably built that they have survived wartime bombing and social change, and remain like fortresses in splendid isolation, the surrounding streets which provided a plentiful supply of large families now demolished. They were built to last, with thick, soundproof walls, high windows out of which no one was ever intended to look, forbidding entrances proclaiming a rigid apartheid of Boys, Girls and Mixed Infants, stone stairs which easily withstood the hammer of steel-capped hobnailed boots, interior décor of shiny tiles impervious to *graffiti*, and — the only concession to the unnecessary — a graceful, cream-coloured cupola visible from terraced-houses round about.

For those who have no memories they are splendid pieces of Victoriana, sensibly designed to fulfil a purpose and with a simple strength and dignity which make them worth at least a passing glance.

The redoubtable men and women who imposed their totalitarian rule on these academic outposts would be horrified by some of the more recent happenings in rooms where their word was law and 'scholars' copied laboriously from blackboards, aware that mistakes would bring painful retribution.

No building in Hull has been such a sensitive barometer of social change over the past century as the school in Brunswick Avenue. Its history began in 1891 when it opened as the Central Higher Grade School, Canon Joseph Malet Lambert's clever ploy to provide something resembling secondary education out of public funds intended for elementary schools. Once free secondary education came officially on the rates,

Brunswick Avenue became the Central Municipal Secondary School, ultimately for girls only, and so remained until 1920 when the girls finally gained access to their purpose-built Newland High School, allowing the boys to move back into what was now the Brunswick Avenue Senior School for Boys. From 1936 it was the premises of the High School and College of Commerce, the College operating in its early years as a night school, the arduous but life-transforming route for school leavers who ended long working days with two or three hours back in a classroom.

Post-war reforms resulted in the expansion of the College and its development as an independent institution with full-time classes. Further education continued to boom and the College of Commerce moved out to a purpose-built block in Queens Gardens. Schools were also in a state of almost permanent revolution: the High School of Commerce was absorbed into the comprehensive system and ceased to exist as a separate entity, leaving Brunswick Avenue (if I've managed to trace all the mutations correctly) for yet another transformation, this time into a newly invented type of school — a junior high.

But that's not the end of the story! Neither Humberside nor Social Services had been conceived when Brunswick Avenue school was designed to the standard plan with a large galleried hall giving access to classrooms on both floors. Now, in its centenary year, it is being converted into headquarters for the — present — County Council's Social Services Department.

Another school of similar layout was created around the same time and not too far away, but for a different clientèle. Hymers College, which has *its* centenary in 1993, was determined to be Hull's leading school for boys and to oust the long-established Grammar School from its traditional role. It began with a distinct advantage, a large and attractive 55-acre site, the former Botanic Gardens, still surrounded by trees and shrubberies and with its ornamental lake.

The first headmaster, C. H. Gore, steered the school towards the pre-eminence that had been its initial aim.

His successor, W. V. Cavill, about whom horror stories abound (with Freudian undertones he signed letters to his relations — 'Will V.C.'), was an autocrat who rejected anything which did not comply with his inflexible ideas. Cavill's totalitarian régime finally ended and, as in post-Stalinist Russia, *glasnost* followed, with three enlightened Heads who introduced a far wider range of subjects and activities and much more tolerant attitudes.

Even more revolutionary, the unthinkable happened, and girls, who did not exist in Cavill's monosexual world, (the few women on the staff had their gender obliterated and were addressed as 'sir'), were admitted, first to the Sixth Form, now to the entire school.

The roof has not collapsed and the dignified red brick building surmounted by the customary cupola of the time, the original school, remains the focal point of a complex of well-designed extensions, surveying the green expanse of the Victorian Botanic Gardens: a typical Hull story of hanging on to the best of the past but accepting that new ideas are a vital part of anything which intends to have a future.

Beverley Road showing Stepney Primary School and swimming baths with large cupola.

Hymers College. Founded by Dr. John Hymers who was Rector of Brandesburton — a fact recalled in nearby Brandesburton Street.

Fountain Road. An attractive school building so typical of many Board schools.

Not a space-ship! The Hi-Tech Perronet Thompson School at Bransholme.

University

Cottingham Road is the nearest Hull gets to a Latin Quarter, more rural and less dashing than its Parisian counterpart but still with an impressive concentration of high I.Q.'s to the inch, and that hint of exhilaration which makes the air of academic institutions so heady. Apart from the University there is Humberside Polytechnic, a quick-change academy which, during 15 hectic years, evolved from College of Education into *Hull* College of Higher Education and soon after that into *Humberside* College of Higher Education. It had

barely transmuted into its present phase as a newly designated polytechnic before the Government announced that such institutions were set to become universities.

The original buildings overlooking the front lawn were ready for use a year before the First World War and have a touch of opulence lacking in the two plain University College buildings opened next door in 1928 when the Edwardian sun had long faded into Depression. Behind them a complex of post-war additions stretches now as far as Inglemire Lane, and the two red-brick blocks have been demoted from the

One of the two original Hull University buildings opened in 1928 with funds generously provided by T. R. Ferens (Chairman of Reckitt's and M.P. for East Hull, 1906-18). Full University status was granted in 1954.

leading roles they played well into the 1950s: one devoted to Arts and the other to Science of the purest kind, for the first Principal did not approve of the Applied variety. Nevertheless, in those early years when universities were scarce, some distinguished teachers and high-quality students were proud to be associated with Hull University College.

In the 1950s it was recovering well from the near fatal impact of war, and expansion began on land at the rear, part of the gift of the founder, T. R. Ferens, a non-graduate who was enthusiastic to give others a privilege denied to himself. Pre-fabs were erected as a temporary measure but by the 1960s growth had gathered unstoppable momentum and humble huts were replaced by clean-lined modern buildings and the towering Brynmor Jones Library raising knowledge to dizzy heights.

This is another part of Hull which has been important to me and which I am unable to see with objective eyes. Buildings change but characters from the past remain in their prime. Like Professor Gillies, always approachable and never at a loss for an anecdote, who stood proprietorially, hands in pockets, on the top step of the Arts block, philosophically

Part of Humberside Polytechnic. A glasshouse on stilts in George Street once the Nautical College — reflecting Hull's strong seafaring tradition.

surveying the world; Dr. Decima Douie, a tiny, frail woman with a formidable brain; Dr. Fred Brooks, spluttering and coughing as he lit his pipe, the archetypal disorganised academic, a distinguished medievalist but a professor *manqué*. Professor Sherard Vines, modern poet and former tutor to the Crown Prince of Japan; Mrs. Margaret 'Espinasse, a strong-minded woman who stood no nonsense; and Miss Rachel Trickett, mellifluous and elegant, who found her métier as Mistress of an Oxford college. But there were many more.

T. R. Ferens' site was eventually inadequate, and the University commandeered roomy houses round about, establishing colonies that continued to grow until the few residents who remained must have felt like native inhabitants of an annexed territory. Telephones, typewriters, microcomputers and bookcases took over best bedrooms, while protest posters in upstairs and downstairs windows left no doubt which houses had been acquired as student accommodation.

Amazingly, in spite of the volume of traffic and its variety of pedestrians, Cottingham Road has not quite

Humberside Polytechnic in Cottingham Road. A fine-looking group of buildings which were formerly Hull Municipal Training College.

lost its original character as a country lane. When the trees on either side are in full leaf there is still a lingering feeling of a rural route between Hull and Cottingham, even more at the approach to Cottingham itself where the road narrows and trees meet overhead in an arched entrance to the village.

Cycling students nowadays travel along Cottingham Road more frequently than horse-drawn vehicles and Hull has, with some reservations, and a certain reluctance, accepted that it is now a university city. On days when degrees are conferred new graduates proudly showing off their gowns and hoods outside the City Hall bring a splash of academic colour into the streets and the ceremonial inside is even more impressive evidence of the status, reputation and influence of Hull.

Universities are no longer ivory towers. Far more local people now have reason to enter the Cottingham Road campus and, provided loss of exclusivity does not mean lowered standards, this closer relationship will be a gain for Gown as well as Town.

The lawned area was once Queen's Dock. It now forms the attractive gardens so well used by lunchtime office workers in summer. The Humberside College of Further Education beyond was originally the Hull Technical College, or 'Tech'.

Central Library

The Central Library in Albion Street is for many people their spiritual home, the building that contains the ever-elusive facts which will one day be revealed and end their obsessional researches into local and family history as triumphantly as Jason's quest for the Golden Fleece.

For others it is a refuge, a waiting room for the homeless, exiles from the 20th century, whiling away the long day which begins when they are turned out of hostels after breakfast with nothing to do but sit incongruously among note-making students and, ever so often, turn over a page of a most unlikely publication — a foreign telephone directory, the *Stock Exchange Year Book* or a later volume of the *Encyclopaedia Britannica* — until eyes relentlessly abandon the pretence of reading and heads begin to droop. Then, suddenly, they flick a page, jerked out of the oblivion that for a few seconds has wiped out weariness.

The original red-brick 1901 library is now only the addendum to the modern part opened in 1962.

All knowledge is here. The well-stocked and well-used Hull Central Library in Albion Street.

Differences between the two sections are more than contrasts of architectural style. In the old building you entered through a dignified hallway, as solemn and admonitory as the vestibule of a church, preparing you for the respect then required of a reader. Borrowing was a privilege and in the earliest days books were far too important to be fingered by the members of the public who had paid for them, and were kept behind bars. Even in modern times frivolity was frowned upon and there were restrictions on the number of novels which could be borrowed.

Libraries now are far more welcoming and informal, with a variety of services never dreamt of when the printed word was unchallenged. Upstairs, the old reference room, converted into the Local Studies Library, remains in all its grandeur, with dark polished panelling and ornate ceiling, traditional in style but catering for a much younger, livelier and more demanding clientèle than the gentlemanly antiquarians of the past. The massively increased interest in local history makes it far too crowded at busy times; yet, less than thirty years ago, it handled all the City's general reference material as well. It has its niche in English Literature. It was here that Winifred Holtby ploughed through the columns of the *Hull Daily Mail* and made notes on events which she incorporated in her greatest novel, *South Riding*, so faintly disguised that her mother, a prominent member of the East Riding County Council, was embarrassed. Winifred's working papers are kept in the library, a fascinating collection for anyone interested in the way a writer's mind works and how fact is turned into fiction.

Some use it now so regularly that it becomes an unofficial club, though its members rarely make conversation. In time they nod and smile in recognition but often have only the vaguest idea what the others are doing: their interests differ but in silence they share the thrill of a detective chase. It is a disciplined, friendly atmosphere, a pleasant environment in which to work, not least because of the helpful, hardworking and efficient staff.

It is a part of Hull where I feel most at home.

Museums

I was taken on a school visit to the museum in Albion Street a short time before it was destroyed in an air raid. Incongruously, bombed-out Thornton-Varley's used the ground floor as a shop, though it seemed perfectly natural at a time when normality was rare. All I

Past life re-created in the newly opened Celtic World exhibition in the Hull and East Riding Museum, High Street.

remember is the highest set of stairs I had ever climbed, and an enormous stuffed bear almost comes into focus. The same afternoon we visited an exhibition of photographs of Dutch reclamation in the Mortimer Gallery at the City Hall, near the British Restaurant where I later ate some truly horrible meals.

Museums then were awesome places (like the marble-halled baronial banks) where you automatically, instinctively lowered your voice, resolved to be on your best behaviour, and never entertained the most fleeting thought of touching the lifeless things enshrined in glass cases.

Even so, Hull Museums were pioneers of progress. Tom Sheppard, appointed Curator in 1901, was determined that his museums should not be mere dumping grounds for ancient rubbish or for embalmed biological freaks more suited to a fairground booth. He organised lectures to bring in the 'working classes' and he was far in advance of his time in planning a piece of three-dimensional history, an old-time street, before the idea was realised in York. Tragically, shortly before he died, his street and the museum in Albion Street were destroyed in the Blitz: his reputation, however, continues to grow as the full extent of his achievement is recognised.

He would have relished the 'Celtic World' exhibition in what is now the Hull and East Riding Museum in High Street. It is a mini-Yorvik, a walk among life-size model people, animals, huts and tree, minus the correct period smells but given a feel of realism by Celtic background noises. Barking dogs and yelling children were just as irritating 2,000 years ago.

Two other traditions have survived. 'The Celtic people of the East Riding were different from their neighbours in the Iron Age,' a notice explains. 'South of the River Humber lived a tribe known as the Coritani or Corieltauvi.' Animosity between North and South Banks apparently has a genetic basis. Perhaps the County of Humberside never had a chance. The exhibition also shows that Celtic males had a penchant for tattoos, a fashion that flourishes more strongly than ever, though artistic standards have declined.

Intricately intertwined patterns revealed more aesthetic sensibility than memorials to 'Dad R.I.P. 1984' or decadent pictures of mermaids and fauna.

Most of us regret being born too soon, a feeling reinforced by 'Celtic World's' reference to Caesar's

So many remember those happy post-war days when the icecream man's bell signalled a real treat, and the shout of, 'Give us some money, Dad!' enchoed down the street. Vehicle in Hull and East Riding Museum, High Street.

A variety of vehicles in the Hull and East Riding Musuem, High Street.

Gallic Wars. Latin may be a dead language but it should never have been relegated to the role of a linguistic corpse whose only purpose was to be dissected into its component parts of speech held together by grammatical rules: the life-destroying way in which it was first presented to me by an atrociously bad 'teacher'. What opportunities were missed! There was never the slightest suggestion that these were real people who had any connection with this area.

Giant Corinthian pillars guard the Hull and East Riding Museum in High Street.

Not far from 'Celtic World' Roman mosaics are displayed in a civilised, villa-like setting. The famous one, discovered at Rudston, has as its centre piece a Venus who looks more like a rag doll than a goddess of desire. In recent times the mosaics have been upstaged by a major find, the Hasholme Boat, which has attracted the attention of the media. The reality is far more impressive than the pictures. It is bigger and blacker than it appears in photographs and, to prevent deterioration, it is unceasingly sprayed in a sealed vapour bath of warm water and wax.

In museums minor items have a habit of staying in the memory as long as the more important. I was interested in a photograph of the bearded Driffield corn merchant, J. R. Mortimer, the amateur archaeologist whose digs would now be frowned on by academics but who created a collection which enhanced the reputation of Hull Museums, its subsequent

owners. And among the vehicles there is G. Stevens and Sons' ice-cream cart. In the post-war period queues formed at their shop for the first taste of a product unavailable for years.

The museum occupies the former Corn Exchange, a building with a grand Victorian facade and a classical pediment depicting Saturn, god of the harvest, accompanied by a selection of agricultural implements. Even grander is the Victorian building now converted into the Town Docks Museum, the triple-domed offices of the Hull Dock Company, also ornate with symbolic stonework, the whole composition a temple to the glory of commerce and a confident statement on the status and future of Hull.

The interior is so rich that it overpowers the exhibits. An imposing staircase, dominated by a thrusting female figure from the prow of a ship, leads to a landing lit by large windows, lightly embossed with the company's logo, 'HDC', in a victor's laurel wreath; then upper flights on either side take you to the first floor which has the magnificent Board Room, a fit venue for 19th-century men of power and property to debate matters of consequence. They took themselves seriously, too seriously at times, but modern decision-makers could do worse than follow their example.

All Hull museums have improved enormously but none more than the Ferens Art Gallery, recently re-opened after the addition of spacious new galleries. It is a beautiful building, with a distinctive appearance, clearly modern but not unconventional, and, inside, a tranquil central hall therapeutically distancing you from the chaos of everyday life and inducing the right frame of mind in which to look at pictures. The Ferens was always a good gallery, but now it is one of the finest in the North of England.

Rembrandt was off when I paid my first visit after the re-opening: not the artist, but a type of chicken sandwich named in his honour. Instead, I opted for Da Vinci, the pictorial name for herring. More space has at last allowed the Ferens to have a restaurant as pleasant as any attached to European galleries, a bonus to art lovers and a blessing to the bored.

These Georgian houses are part of the Wilberforce Museum in High Street.

A Visit to High Street and Wilberforce House is a 'must' for all visitors to Hull.

Top Right — Young explorers looking at history in an attractive way as they clamber across the finely renovated Beverley Gate.

Middle Right — The Beverley Gate at Monument Bridge. The scene of a great event in Hull's history as shown on explanatory boards.

Bottom Right — The Town Docks Museum with its fishing history stares haughtily down at the metal and glass of modern upstart Princes Quay. The giant bollards once held mighty ships in place in Princes Dock.

New Buildings

Hull had a lucky escape.

Architecture was in the doldrums for more than two decades after the war and these were the years when blitzed buildings tottered into even greater dereliction, when weeds and plants grew unhindered on bombsites still scarring the centre, and declining areas declined even further.

Fortunately, few important new buildings appeared, and, though there was much muttering about disgraceful delays, Hull was not disfigured by the insensitive structures that soon became the eyesores of other cities. Of course, there were failures and lost opportunities when disappointing buildings were put up on too prominent sites, but by the time Hull stirred into vigorous activity and rejuvenation, architects had learnt their lesson and were trying to design buildings showing some understanding of the existing style and historic character of the environment of which they were to form a part.

The revival of brickwork suited Hull, for this was its traditional building material, and Hull, after all, has its place in national history as the one brick-built town of the Middle Ages. New housing, which finally reversed the exodus of a resident population from the Old Town, was neatly apposite, and usually avoided the dinkiness favoured by heritage-obsessed conservationists.

Listing good modern buildings is a certain way to arouse controversy. The gut-reactions of people who 'know what they like' are often nearer the mark than aesthetic judgements of those who claim to be experts, provided that first impressions are not infallibly regarded as final impressions. Buildings have a habit of growing more or less beautiful with the passing of time.

I like the Polytechnic building in George Street (lots of glass and straight lines but bright and positive), the Postgraduate Medical School at the Infirmary (up-to-date but well mannered, as you would expect from a good G.P. who keeps in touch with the latest developments), and the new Law Courts (a subtle blend of modernity and tradition, like the English legal system itself). Otherwise undistinguished buildings sometimes have eye-catching features, and even a multi-storey car park can redeem itself by the geometric pattern of its concrete curves. Buildings which fulfil their intended function with the minimum of fuss can have a simplicity and a dignity which verge on beauty.

The very latest developments are too new to evaluate but not difficult to identify: cinemas, restaurants, ice-rink, factories and superstores in strong and sometimes aggressive style, their decorative features equally primitive, in eye-blasting shades of blue, red, green and yellow, loud enough to attract attention even if placed among the gaudy glamour of Walton Street fairground.

Some are really nothing more than huge sheds, so

The multiscreen Odeon Cinema on the St. Andrew's Quay development.

Car parks aplenty on St. Andrew's Quay.

The Megabowl on Fisherman's Wharf, St. Andrew's Quay.

St. Andrew's Quay where history is preserved in bollards off the car park.

The Ice Rink in Kingston Street is the home of the successful Sea Hawks Ice Hockey Team.

plain and uncompromising that they stir memories of the Brutalist architecture of Germany in the Thirties. They are purpose-built and no doubt relatively cheap and quickly erected, but they're also monolithic and, for me at least, menacing, built on a scale far too vast for humans to feel at ease inside them.

One thing they have in common probably has deep significance, though its precise import eludes me. Outwardly — apart from their names — there is little to distinguish factories from buildings intended for pleasure. (Industrial and business *parks* have also appropriated a name previously associated with public gardens.) At the turn of the century extravagantly embellished cinemas like the Tower were created as magical palaces with hints of the Arabian Nights, offering an evening in a dream world far more enthralling than the one left outside in Anlaby Road.

These new factory-look-alikes may be carrying a coded message that there is no essential difference between work and play: how you spend your time is your own affair — moral absolutes do not exist. The demarcation between work and leisure time has been fudged in so many ways. Hull weekends now begin early on Friday afternoon, not the Saturday midday which, well into the Fifties, marked the finish of another week of work and the start of real living. Flat caps are now club comics' stage props, and bib and brace overalls and lace-up boots have been replaced by jeans, T-shirts and trainers, the all-purpose ensemble for work and pleasure. It *must* mean something!

Out-of-town 8-screen cinemas showing the latest releases with almost unlimited parking for patrons who are expected to come by car also exist in a different dimension from the pre-television world where people used public transport, stood expectantly in long queues, sometimes in the rain and, at last, experienced the near orgasmic climax of the moment when the commissionnaire, dressed like a Ruritanian officer, admitted them to the foyer to pay 1/9d and, after a torch-led fumble through the sudden total blackness, to achieve their objective and be one of those privileged to see the film that everyone in Hull was talking about.

Law Courts

We went into the new Law Courts through the tradesmen's entrance. Judge Jack Walker had kindly agreed to arrange a guided tour during the lunch-time adjournment; the possibility of taking a photograph inside had been discussed but courts and photographers do not mix in an age of high security, and the bleeping of senior staff and a phone call to a regional office were unproductive.

In the court where Judge Walker was still sitting the atmosphere was quiet, intimate and conversational, with the few participants grouped in front of the bench, watched only by the fewer spectators affected by the outcome. Acoustics were perfect and no one needed to raise his voice: adversarial histrionics would have been in poor taste.

It was the second day of a complicated case concerning a woman who had stood security for a bank loan to her husband. The day of reckoning had arrived and now the bank official who had arranged the matter was in the witness box being politely, relentlessly, grilled about the exact words he had used: the issue was whether the wife, now widowed, had understood what she was undertaking. He answered slowly and painstakingly, admitting that the precise words were past recall, and at one point Judge Walker intervened sympathetically: these events had occurred seven years previously, he reminded the cross-examining barrister.

The case was conducted in a professional, civilised manner. Law can be an emotional battleground, but the new building has a tranquil, calming interior with its subdued décor of pink and grey, its deep-pile carpets which deaden sound, and its light spaciousness.

To a first-time visitor taken along an unaccustomed route behind the scenes the building is confusing, though simple geometry lies beneath the superficial complexity. In essence it is round, a series of concentric circles, with a grand concourse like a posh hotel's, and an artistically sculpted white marble staircase curving to the first floor where numbered courts radiate from this central hub, a circular waiting area with round banquettes. Behind the courts is an outer circle corridor, with a variety of rooms for staff, officials and police on the perimeter.

The courts occupy a superb site near the junction of major roads, and inevitably those working in the front rooms have as a perk some of the finest views in the City. Luckiest of all are the ones who occupy an office not far from St. Mary's Church looking towards the Edwardian Imperial architecture of the Post Office, along Alfred Gelder Street with the magnificent Italianate facade of the Guildhall and — the crowning bonus — a commanding view of the Guildhall's Lowgate entrance which will surely make the room a popular venue whenever a member of the Royal Family pays an official visit to Hull.

Seeing the parts others cannot see is particularly enjoyable for those of us who are inquisitive. It also boosts one's ego to enter a court room by the door usually reserved for the judge, and there are other privileges: a close-up view of the judicial wig deposited upside down on a table, in another room the individually named neat tin boxes for barristers' wigs, and walking round a metal catwalk at the summit of the building and looking up at the wooden lining of the dome, designed to harmonise with other domes on the City skyline.

Quite apart from its legal function, the building is a bastion of good spoken English, a place where language is used with the precision and care it deserves. Sloppiness and ambiguity can have costly consequences. Here, every word counts.

The Law Courts also embody a characteristic which may not be unique to this country but is a prominent feature of our history. Inside this up-to-the-minute building incorporating every modern facility, the rules, precedents and traditions of law are observed as respectfully as ever they were. One of the great lessons of English history is the way stability has been secured by honouring the past while responding to changing needs. The Hull Law Courts are an encouraging symbol of the durability of the best features of our national life.

*The impressive and attractively designed Law Courts at the junction of
Alfred Gelder Street and Lowgate.*

Survivals

Odd buildings which have outlived all the changes and developments and linger on, nudged by slicker, more thrusting modern neighbours, like people who have lived too long, or stand in an isolation of waste, like ships that have beached and will never sail again.

Park Row, off Park Street, has the solid four-square house that belonged to Alderman John Symons, jeweller, silversmith, journalist and early local historian. Incongruous among the 20th-century industrial complexes of Wincolmlee, a homely cottage just about manages to hold its own, and Bridge End Cottage, Inglemire Lane, is a remarkable survival of a Georgian country cottage, surrounded by modern buildings, a rural oasis in a city suburb with a never-ending stream of traffic rushing past its pleasant garden. Above modern shop and office facades there's a different Hull of perfectly proportioned windows, graceful pediments and sophisticated ornamentation.

Some of it is positively grand, like the upper storeys of Boots the Chemist in Whitefriargate, originally the premises of the Neptune Inn, opened in 1797 and still displaying the insignia of its owners, Trinity House, along with a varied collection of nautical symbols. The Neptune never succeeded in becoming Hull's most fashionable inn, the role for which it was so confidently intended. In 1815 it began a new phase of public service as the Custom House. When Boots took over the building the spacious first-floor banqueting room housed their subscription library, a long-lost amenity which gave polite pleasure and refined reassurance to readers too timid to enter a public library. Now it is used as a staff room, though open to the public once a year on a Saturday in July as part of the City Council's Civic Programme. Entrance is by a wooden staircase at the side of the shop, and, in spite of all the signs of current use — not to be criticised, for buildings are more likely to survive if they continue to fulfil a purpose —, you can, with a little imagination, remove the modern furniture and appreciate the grand scale on which it was conceived. Crane your neck and gaze up at the ceiling's formally patterned plasterwork, and, best of all, look down Parliament Street towards Queens Gardens and view an inspired bit of Georgian planning. Once the first dock was opened in 1778 on Hull's northern boundary, easy access from the Old Town was essential, and so Parliament Street was cut through to provide a link. As well as being more convenient it enabled the *glitterati* of Georgian Hull to stand at the

Bridge Cottage, Inglemire Lane, a rare survival.

Parliament Street — a dignified street of offices, once a 'good address' for prosperous residents.

upper windows of the Neptune and admire a picturesque vista as they looked along the civilised terraces of Parliament Street and rested their eyes on the ships which brought them their wealth and their privileged status.

Boots, Marks & Spencer, Woolworth, and all the other famous national and international stores have instantly identifiable house styles and facias which make the shops in Hull no different from those elsewhere. Hull buses, on the other hand, now come in a variety of colours, even rhubarb and custard, but the result is the same: a dent in the city's corporate identity symbolised by the blue and white which returning natives always recognised as a welcome sign that they were back on home territory. Most people feel reassured by familiar sights, which suggest stability; repeated changes disorientate. Familiar buses, bus stops and bus routes provide a reliable way through a confusing life: Hull people find it heartening to recall the numbers of the trolley buses (61, 62, 63 and so on) and demonstrate their feats of memory on the routes they served and the cost of a ticket in that golden age before money lost its value.

Grammar School Hard. New housing at the back of the surviving old Grammar School building (right) — now a museum.